COLLEGE ADMISSIONS TOGETHER

COLLEGE ADMISSIONS TOGETHER

It Takes a Family

Steven Roy Goodman, MS, JD
Andrea Leiman, PhD

CAPITAL IDEAS SERIES

CAPITAL
BOOKS, INC.
Sterling, Virginia

Capital Books, Inc.
P.O. Box 605
Herndon, Virginia 20172-0605

ISBN: 978-1-933102-54-2 (alk. paper)

Library of Congress Cataloging-in-Publication Data

Goodman, Steven Roy.
College admissions together : it takes a family / Steven Roy Goodman, Andrea Leiman.
p. cm. — (Capital ideas series)
ISBN-13: 978-1-933102-54-2 (alk. paper)
1. College choice—United States. 2. Universities and colleges—United States—Admission. 3. Education, Higher—Parent participation—United States. I. Leiman, Andrea. II. Title.
LB2350.5.G66 2007
378.1'610973—dc22

2007020189

Printed in the United States of America on acid-free paper that meets the American National Standards Institute Z39-48 Standard.

First Edition

10 9 8 7 6 5 4 3 2 1

To Jenny and Mia, our extended family, and the many college-bound students and their families I have had the pleasure to know.

—S.R.G.

To Paul, with whom I navigated the college years and beyond; and to Lauren, David, and Jonathan, who have made this journey a joy.

—A.L.

Contents

Foreword

As a Beverly Hills High School college counselor, I talk with students every day about how to achieve their college aspirations, their plans to succeed in various academic programs, and their interest in preparing for specific careers.

Parents usually talk with me about the same things, but I often wonder if the parents are talking about the same children who came to see me a day or two before. A sophomore will tell me at the beginning of the week how badly she wants to explore film in college and possibly try her hand at serious movie-making. The father will then come to see me later in the week to explain how committed his daughter is to studying accounting and the business aspects of the film industry.

My job as a counselor is to help reconcile these student-parent differences. I can't split every decision down the middle and please all of the families in Beverly Hills all of the time. I can, however, encourage my students and their parents to sit down and talk. I urge them to really listen to each other's needs and desires. Then our conversations about college applications, prospective majors, and possible careers become a lot more productive.

This is why the family roadmap you have in your hands is so valuable. Educational consultant Steve Goodman, whom I have known for more than twenty years, is one of the country's leading college and graduate school admissions advisors. He has teamed up in this book with family psychologist and professor Dr. Andrea Leiman, who has devoted her professional career to strengthening parent-child relationships.

Together they give you a fourteen-chapter head start that will make your family's college admissions journey as painless as possible. *College Admissions Together: It Takes a Family* will help you, your spouse, and your child carefully begin the college search and work productively until the admissions decisions roll in.

I'm from California, so I can get away with encouraging you to relax. By looking at the admissions process as a family, listening to one another, recognizing your different goals and expectations, and coming to understand why your son or daughter (or your husband or wife, for that matter) is thinking or behaving in a particular way, you can successfully move through the admissions process as a team.

So read, take notes, and follow the guidance in this book. Appreciate the productive time that you will now be able to share with your family during the college admissions process. Take these admissions and psychological insights to heart and apply them directly to your family today.

HANNA ZYLBERBERG
COLLEGE COUNSELOR
BEVERLY HILLS HIGH SCHOOL

Preface

This book will help you and your family lay the foundation for a successful, conflict-minimizing college search. We address the realities of today's
college admissions process and suggest ways that the process itself can become a source of family bonding. By addressing the major educational and
developmental factors that influence most college searches, you'll find that
both you and your family will face less conflict and that your child will improve her chances of finding and being admitted to the schools of her choice.

Profound emotional and family issues tend to rise to the surface during the college search. In *College Admissions Together*, we first look at the psychology of teenagers in general and provide you with insights that will help
you examine your child's behavior in particular. Then we consider the key
factors affecting parents at this transitional point in their lives—and what
you'll need to know about yourself that will affect your family's successful
completion of the college admissions process. Finally, we explore the dynamics at play within the family and beyond. This includes your extended family
members, friends, and acquaintances, as well as other social influences.

Most cultures have a rite of passage that marks a child's entry to adulthood and assumption of mature responsibilities. In American society, the cultural rite of passage is often marked by leaving for college. Decisions about
looking at colleges, applying to various institutions, and leaving home exacerbate tension within the family. How a family addresses these specific college

admissions matters, as well as underlying developmental issues, is crucial to both a successful college selection outcome and a well-adjusted family in the future.

All families approach the coming of age of their teenagers in different ways. The college search and application process merely increases the tensions already present in a family during this stage of the life cycle. Despite the infinite variations on the theme of adolescent maturation, there are clear steps that you and your family can take during this period to avoid the danger zones while enhancing your family's relationships. Of course, we can't help you avoid all family conflict. Rather, we suggest ways to constructively discuss emotionally charged issues and offer you our knowledge and years of experience to help resolve family conflict during this exciting and challenging transition.

STEVEN ROY GOODMAN, MS, JD

ANDREA LEIMAN, PhD

Acknowledgments

We would like to thank the families we have counseled over the past two decades. We are grateful to the students, parents, grandparents, aunts, uncles, teachers, school counselors, admissions officers, and athletic coaches who have confided in us. Through their trust, we have helped to launch thousands of teenagers to college.

For us, the greatest rewards of the admissions process happen when students find the right schools and families look back at having worked together as a team along the way. In the spirit of passing along what we have learned, we share with you our collective experiences and insights about families and the college admissions process.

STEVEN ROY GOODMAN, MS, JD
ANDREA LEIMAN, PHD

Introduction

In our combined forty years of experience working with adolescents and families, we have witnessed firsthand how the college admissions process can either go critically wrong—or right, resulting in exciting, positive outcomes. Some families seem to glide through the college search and application process while others are adrift and seemingly rudderless. Families who don't address the profound educational and emotional issues that arise during this period run the risk of permanently damaging family relationships, as well as failing the admissions process—namely, not finding a good college match.

We recognize the frightening aspects of this journey. Those of you who may have gone through it already with one or more children, or those of you who are novices, know that the anticipation of dealing with so many variables can be daunting. We know what it's like to prepare for this endeavor, and that's why *College Admissions Together* will help you and your family through the journey.

Traversing the college admissions landscape can be an overwhelming undertaking—not just for students, but for families as well. Gaining admission to selective colleges and universities parallels the increased complexity and competitiveness of the job market and our society. Water-cooler discussions abound regarding the best means for teens to gain entrance to their first-choice college. However, in frantically chasing after the elusive numbers that many people believe will ensure admission to highly ranked educational institutions, families often ignore deep-rooted personal issues stirred up by the college search.

Many of you have been diligently doing your homework, reading up on how to gain admission to the best school for your child. In this book, we take you a step further—we provide you with the tools necessary to proceed *emotionally* during this critical period. With a deep appreciation of the admissions process, we've seen families emerge from the college search happier than ever before. Not only were they thrilled with the college choices open to their sons or daughters in April of senior year, but they also came through the experience with a closer sense of family connection and caring and a greater understanding and appreciation of one another as individuals.

Many families have the misconception that getting into college is a totally linear function. You set a goal, you establish what you need to do to reach that goal, and then you (or more likely, your child) follow those prescribed steps. While understanding the mechanics of what has to occur is crucial, we want you, the parent, to understand the emotional aspects as well.

We want to emphasize how important it is for your family to operate in a unified, positive manner. Think of your family sitting together in a rowboat. If each family member has an oar but rows independently, the boat will probably just go in circles. You'll have a much better chance of moving forward if your family works together. Not only will you improve the chances of your student finding the right schools, but all of you will be able to enjoy the ride and ultimately arrive at the same happy destination together.

We'll help you gain a greater understanding of the family developmental issues that arise during your student's high school years. Whether this is the first teenager you are raising or the fifth, you know that living with an adolescent can be nerve-wracking. You are not alone in this endeavor—there are more than twenty million teenagers between the ages of fourteen and nineteen in the United States.

A key to successfully navigating this difficult period and to minimizing conflict during the admissions process is to use the depth and breadth of your knowledge about your own child to smooth out the rough spots. The more you understand your child, the easier it will be to focus your teenager's college search. With improved channels of communication, you can confidently set more realistic expectations about timelines, responsibilities, and general family discussions.

What makes this period so confounding is the fact that teenagers are constantly changing, and you don't always know how they're going to act or what they will focus on. One morning your adolescent may resemble a toddler more than a young adult, but the very next day she may be supremely mature and responsible. This is tricky enough to manage under the best of circumstances, but when you factor in having to develop a long-range plan for gaining admission to college or preparing for a particular career, this can lead to tremendous stress and anxiety for everyone.

Adolescents constantly struggle to develop a sense of autonomy and independence. Just as your teenager is trying to create greater distance, literally and figuratively, from you, you'll be needing to flex some of your parental authority in overseeing the application process. We discuss in this book how you can respect your child's need for some separation but at the same time collaborate to ensure that college applications are submitted in a timely fashion. It's an important developmental concept that children don't need to be totally independent of their families—and it's healthy to acknowledge a mutually respectful interdependence. The college admissions process presents an excellent opportunity to work toward this goal.

The condition of being an adolescent usually involves a degree of angst and unhappiness; it's the nature of being a teenager. However, this awareness rarely alleviates your parental frustration and distress because you don't know what, if anything, you can do to make your child's discomfort go away. When you add college admissions stress to the equation, everyone in the family runs the risk of being unhappy, angry, or even depressed.

A proactive approach to college admissions will ensure a healthier transition to college for your student as well as for those family members left behind. *College Admissions Together* sheds light on critical characteristics of the admissions process that should be addressed long before applications are submitted. We discuss important matters embedded in the college search and how they interact with developmental issues. We focus on aspects of the college admissions process that tend to elicit family conflict. For example, how do college essays get written? How much input should parents have? What about your child's tendencies toward procrastination?

We address a number of problematic situations that usually arise during the college admissions process, including:

▸ *Unfolding family strife and emotional tension.* The stressful nature of the admissions process can lead to disagreements among family members, including siblings and grandparents. Everyone in your extended family chimes in with opinions. We offer strategies to help contain those other voices and reduce family conflict.

▸ *External pressures.* Today's college admissions process has become a long-term, time-consuming family endeavor. Many high school students and families spend years of time and energy focused on college, which may conflict with other time demands such as job and school responsibilities, sibling needs, and students' extracurricular activities. We carefully explore ideas for managing various pressures.

▸ *Resurgence of hostilities between you and your child.* This book helps you avoid estrangement from your teenager during the college admissions process. We explain how to use this period to strengthen the relationships within your family. (A style note: to be as fair and representative as possible, we have alternated the use of "he" and "she" when discussing situations involving teenagers.)

We examine how you and your family can handle the waiting period from January to April and how to fully enjoy the months before final decisions need to be made. Not only is this a good time to sit back and enjoy one another, but if you use this time well, it will also help lay the groundwork for the important physical, emotional, and pre-professional transitions that lie ahead.

Our interest in college admissions and the nature of family relationships during the college admissions process has grown out of our many years of professional experience. Steven Roy Goodman, an internationally recognized educational consultant, has counseled more than 1,500 college-bound students and families during the past eighteen years. He helps students strengthen their college and graduate school admissions market positions by advising them about admissions strategies and essay preparation. Andrea Leiman is a clinical psychologist and professor with more than twenty-five years of experience working with families in psychotherapy. In addition to maintaining her private practice, she lectures and consults regularly with parent groups and schools. Our collaboration on this book offers a way to help families emerge from the college admissions process feeling like they have achieved a major life goal together.

1

A Safe Passage to Adulthood

How do you make college decisions together when all your teenager wants is independence?

Transitional periods always involve some degree of stress, and adolescence is not an exception to this rule. Whenever there is a major shift in the family structure, such as the birth of a new baby or one child leaving home for college, the family organization becomes strained. Any group experiences its greatest tension when members enter or leave. Stress can be a mentally or emotionally disruptive influence that taxes the individual's and family's resources. For most parents, anticipating an adolescent's departure from home can be emotionally draining.

What makes the college admissions process a potential danger zone for families is the confluence of issues happening at the same time. While critical decisions need to be made as a family about the future of the college-bound member, families are in the midst of coping with his or her burgeoning independence.

It is developmentally appropriate for your son or daughter sometimes to be distant and at other times to move closer to you. Teenagers play out the same themes from their toddlerhood. When they learn to walk, children experiment by walking away from their parents—and then return for support and guidance a few minutes later. Your teenager is also experimenting with separation, yet at the same time, he continues to need reassurance and connection to family.

The crucial question for you as a parent is how do I stay involved with my child while allowing him to literally and emotionally gain distance from the family?

We understand the dilemma you're facing, as you try to figure out when to ask questions and when to back off. For example, maybe your teenager has been brushing off your questions about college. Has he been dragging his feet about setting up a preliminary meeting with his school counselor?

Just as you needed to encourage your toddler to take his first baby steps, even with the risk of tumbling down, you also need to be supportive of your teenager's steps toward adulthood. Yet, as with your toddler, you need to stay close to provide support and protection when it's needed.

What if your teen says, "It's none of your business," but then you find out from other parents that there's a meeting at school for parents and students that he never even told you about?

Your task as a parent during this period is to recognize when to give your child some room and when to rein him back in. Sometimes it makes sense to just let an early deadline slip if—and this is a big if—your child will come to understand it's his admissions process and that he needs to take ownership of it. In general, it's useful to think about giving your child choices. For instance, you can explain that he needs to attend an upcoming college fair. He can choose to go with or without you and then can select the most convenient fair of his choice—but he does need to go.

In addition to grappling with adolescent developmental issues, you may experience your son or daughter's impending departure for college as a developmental marker: the end of your active parenting days. For some parents, this may seem like a relief. For others, there may be a deep sense of loss. Wherever you may find yourself on this continuum, you should remember that families are forever: you always remain your child's parent.

For those of you looking forward to selling the house or reconfiguring your child's bedroom; be forewarned. Don't do it right away. Your child will still feel it is her home and will want a familiar place to which to return. And for those of you anticipating a loss, you should also remember that your teenager will *want* to come home.

How you navigate the budding independence and adulthood of your teenager does not signal the end of the parent-child relationship. Rather, it sets the groundwork for the next developmental stage of your family. When successful, this complicated process can lead to a mutually rewarding relationship that lasts a lifetime. The goal of this next developmental stage is to find that balance between you and your child where you can treat one another in an adult, caring, mutually supportive, and respectful manner.

> ~The goal of this next developmental stage is to find that balance between you and your child where you can treat one another in an adult, caring, mutually supportive, and respectful manner. ~

An example of this is how Madison, a recent high school graduate, and her parents used the pre-college phase to develop mutual respect and a better communication style. Together, they deliberately worked on ways to resolve conflicts. They negotiated differences about distance from home and size of the student body. Now that she's settled at school, Madison regularly keeps in touch with her parents, and all seem to enjoy the conversations. While she is happily ensconced at college, she is also happy to come home during breaks and to spend time with her family.

This developmental dilemma is played out during the college application process as you, the parent, determine ways to stay involved while allowing your child to make more choices. While engaged in admissions procedures, you might discover that family interaction patterns are already taking on new characteristics. Who makes decisions about your teenager's activities, schoolwork, social life, extracurricular activities, and time spent with the family may all be in flux.

In the past you probably scheduled all your child's activities, including sports, music lessons, and play dates. Now your teenager not only decides what she wants to do, but also when and with whom. You used to be able to say, "Go do your homework." Now you may find your student doing her homework at midnight while listening to music.

Perhaps holidays were always considered family time. Now your daughter wants to spend spring break with her best friend rather than with your family. In general, you used to know in much greater detail what was going on in your child's life. Now you're probably lucky if you know the names of more than five of your daughter's friends.

Remain an active parent during the high school years, even if your child acts as if she doesn't want this. By staying involved and engaged, you lay the groundwork for positive future family relationships as well as prepare the way for a successful college admissions search. Your goal here should be to help your child become an independent adult safely, with a solid family base to return to as needed.

Part of a safe passage to adulthood involves helping your child to choose the right college for her. Not having a clear understanding of your child's daily activities can have a detrimental effect on both your family dynamics and the admissions process. If your teenager is not regularly sharing her life with you, you may not have access to vital information such as college fair dates, test-filing deadlines, required courses, and meetings with admissions personnel.

DIFFERENT WORLDVIEWS

What makes the admissions process maddening for many families is the intersection of a teen's incomplete knowledge with his newfound need to be an active decision maker in plans that will affect his future. We encourage you to show respect for your student's wants and needs, even if they strike you as outrageous.

Like many parents, you probably have different perspectives on the world than your teenager. Having greater real-life experiences, however, is only one reason why your worldview will differ from your child's. What makes you comfortable may be completely different from what makes your son or daughter comfortable. As an example, while you, if in your child's shoes, would want to be close to family and things that are familiar, your teenager may crave adventure and have a strong drive to explore. Can you accept this difference? Can you learn to feel okay with your child's choices—as long as they are relatively thoughtful and safe? Are you able to even envision your teenager as an adult?

Sometimes the preferences your teenager states are unrealistic and anything but adultlike. His choices may be incompatible. It's not uncommon for students to declare that they want to attend a college or university with extremely small classes but that also has a Division I football team and 20,000 students with whom to socialize.

A frequent conflict involves underachieving students and demanding parents. Unfortunately, oil and water don't mix. In such a situation, it's difficult to respect each other's views and agree on a strategy. You want to respect your child, but you know that he still needs to become more invested in his own education.

At many points in the process, you and your teenager are likely to disagree, whether it's about when to write application essays and how many times to revise them, or about how many colleges to apply to. You don't have to agree with your son or daughter, but you'll move the process forward if you learn to disagree respectfully. A first necessary step is to be able to listen to your child's needs and wants. Again, this can be difficult when your child wants something quite different than you do, which may occur often. But if you've practiced hearing him out and tried your best to understand what he wants or needs, you'll be able to react calmly and rationally when, for example, he suggests applying only to Harvard because, after all, that's the only school he is willing to attend.

> ∽ You don't have to agree with your son or daughter, but you'll move the process forward if you learn to disagree respectfully. ∽

To help address these dilemmas, we recommend three exercises: (1) role reversal, (2) parental motivations, and (3) listening. The benefits of these exercises may not be evident while you're doing them, but they can have big payoffs in the long term. Along the way, make sure to treat your proud, independence-seeking adolescent with respect. Without that, communication will likely be unproductive or come to a halt altogether. To get through the college admissions process, you need to keep the lines of communication open at all times.

Exercise 1: Role Reversal 101

Arrange time for a family role-reversal exercise so that everyone can come to appreciate one another's views. Consider where you want to do this. For some families, the living room may be perfectly comfortable. Other families find that a neutral setting, such as a restaurant or a library, is more conducive to this delicate conversation.

Each family member should prepare in advance a list of twenty colleges that might be of interest and five aspects of colleges that appear to be most desirable.

At the time of the discussion, you should take out your lists and give them to your child. Have your child give you hers. Take a few minutes to read and digest what is on it, and then begin the role-reversal exercise by having one of you defend the other's college positions.

Plan ahead by giving some thought to your child's possible college choices. You should ask your child to do the same and prepare to take your position about various colleges. Students who have been active in organizations like Model United Nations usually have little difficulty in trying to defend opposing positions. Other students, however, may need a little coaching. The exercise, though awkward, is well worth it. Through the role-reversal, students and parents are forced to see the strengths and weaknesses of their own views and the intensity with which other family members agree or disagree. Additionally, the exercise tends to reduce the likelihood of polarized positions. By articulating other people's positions and seeing the world through their eyes, it is easier to understand their points of view.

Exercise 2: Parental Motivations

The second exercise is just for you, as a parent. We encourage you to speak with other parents directly—without students—about your motivating factors behind particular college-related decisions. It's okay to find out what's on the minds of others and explore how your friends view the college admissions process. Sit down with them, away from home, and list the issues that are most important to you regarding college choice. Have them do the same thing. Then compare notes and discuss why you took particular positions.

This exercise will help you to prioritize factors and see that other mothers and fathers are experiencing similar issues. It's useful to talk not only with parents who are going through the same stage but also with parents who may have different perspectives on the process.

Exercise 3: How to Listen to Be Understood

The goal of this exercise is to help both you and your teen understand the underpinnings of your own frame of reference and make it easier to see and hear different viewpoints about the college decision-making process.

Specifically, this exercise involves learning how to be an active listener. That means focusing fully on what someone is saying to you and responding constructively after the speaker is finished making his point. We'll return to this exercise several times. You can apply it to many situations you will encounter with your teenager. It requires selecting a time and place that is relatively stress-free and comfortable.

You may want to use a stopwatch for the first several times you try this exercise. We have found that it's easier to tolerate shorter periods of hearing what you may not want to hear. Use uninterrupted three-minute intervals for each family member to explain what he or she is looking for during and at the end of the college admissions process. After one person finishes, the next person summarizes the previous person's comments. Make sure that every family member gets to express his or her personal views. Be careful not to interrupt your child during her three minutes. Students, in particular, like to know that they are being heard.

This active listening exercise gives teenagers and parents the opportunity to think through and explain their views in an uninterrupted way. This is critical so that your student feels validated and important—even if she says, "What do you mean, what am I looking for through the college admissions process? I just want to get into college."

The underlying principle of active listening is that you are validating the other person's perspective while not necessarily agreeing with it. This reduces polarization, minimizes conflict, and paves the way for developing consensus.

No matter how good your current relationship may be with your child, there will always be some level of tension regarding the when, where, and how of allowing your child to behave independently. The rule of thumb suggests that the readiness for adulthood comes about two years later than your adolescent claims and about two years before you will admit. Thus,

> ～The rule of thumb suggests that the readiness for adulthood comes about two years later than your adolescent claims and about two years before you will admit. ～

there is an intrinsic psychological and emotional struggle, which is played out and highlighted during the college admissions process.

This struggle plays out most frequently with parents who are concerned that their child is not mature enough to make sound decisions regarding college selection. Often parents contact us to explain their choices of the ideal colleges for their children—even if their son or daughter has expressly indicated a preference for different types of colleges.

The opposite scenario also occurs often. In this case, a child unequivocally declares that her mediocre grades and current study habits will become a thing of the past the minute she goes off to college and is on her own. The extreme case of this is the student who asserts, "I'm an adult. Let me make my own decisions," thereby refusing to allow her parents to contribute.

Teenagers are like sand on a beach. They are ever-changing yet constant. At one moment, they have boundless energy, and the next, they are exhausted for what seems to be days on end. One minute they exude supreme confidence, and the next, they are a ball of insecurities. Sometimes they behave as if they never want to see their families again, but later they may revert to wanting snuggle time with parents.

Your student's motivation will wax and wane. Some days your child will be extremely enthusiastic about the prospects of her upcoming college experience. Other days, she may be disinterested, feeling consumed with more immediate concerns. Her specific academic interests are also likely to shift. More than 60 percent of American students who declare a particular major on their application end up graduating with a different major. These shifts occur even more frequently during high school. Your daughter may want to go to art school, but later reconsider and decide to pursue a liberal arts degree.

The shifting makes it quite difficult to plan. If your child's focus keeps changing, it's very hard to pursue a path toward a particular goal. Among other things, such shifting has an impact on visiting college campuses and test-taking schedules. You can't visit twenty universities in one weekend.

We advise families to talk, talk, talk, and then talk some more—up to a point. The message should be that it's good to consider as many options as possible, but as a parent you may need to cut off discussion at some finite time in the future.

There's an element here of going with the flow. You can actually enjoy your child's adolescent behavior to a point and assert yourself only when and if your child can't come to a resolution on her own.

Adolescents are notorious for being reluctant to plan ahead or anticipate possible consequences of their behavior. For example, suggesting that students need to worry about their academic performance in ninth grade because it might affect their ability to gain admission to the college of their choice three years later, may be viewed as an absurd parental position.

DEVELOPMENTAL PRESSURES

Many teenagers struggle to remain close to their families while also beginning to create some distance. It's not remarkable that adolescents can seem like two-year-olds, uncertain and ambivalent about pulling away from their parents and also wanting to remain close. Just as toddlers are in a state of developmental transition when they recognize their separateness from their parents, adolescents are caught between wanting to remain children and attempting to stake out their independence, maturity, and young adulthood.

While you need to set appropriate parental limits, be sure to avoid generalizing your child's need for oversight to all situations, including college admissions tasks. Perhaps your daughter regresses to childhood once a day and whines that she needs you to make her a snack or throws a minor tantrum when the only dress that doesn't make her look fat is dirty, or whatever. This is likely to make you start nagging her more than you were inclined to about her college essay writing because you have inadvertently turned back into the mother of an eight-year-old in response to your daughter's behavior.

~As we have been stressing, your first job as a parent is to be aware of these developmental pressures. If you know what may be coming down the road, you can be better prepared both emotionally and strategically.~

As we have been stressing, your first job as a parent is to be aware of these developmental pressures. If you know what may be coming down the road, you can be better prepared both emotionally and strategically.

Another dimension of your teenager's developing adulthood involves physical growth. Despite teenagers' apparent physical maturation, they are still kids. They often want to feel all grown up and ready to cut the emotional cords. But simultaneously, they may yearn for the comfort and security of parents and family. Learning a new role—moving from child to young adult —is stressful, exciting, and frightening. They do, in fact, have the need to feel safe and the urge to be free.

In the context of college admissions, the emotional passage to adult-hood involves the resolution of a concrete problem: selecting a place to go to college. Working together toward a solution is a finely choreographed dance that each family must learn. You need to figure out how to encourage your adolescent to confidently move on emotionally while maintaining a founda-tion of nurturance and support.

TAKING STOCK

There's an old saying that there are two valuable gifts that parents can give their children: roots and wings. Parents hope that, throughout their child's development, they have provided the roots of security, unconditional love, and stability. When teenagers are preparing to leave the nest, parents can support them as they try their wings and work toward physical independence and emotional interdependence.

Preparing teenagers to leave the nest requires family reorganization, which can be painful. You need to balance your willingness and ability to let your child go with staying connected.

Ask yourself a number of questions that will help you determine your comfort zone in launching your teenager to young adulthood. Can you imag-ine yourself:

▸ Taking a weeklong vacation without your child?

▸ Not speaking directly to your daughter for more than a week?

▸ Dropping your child off at college and then going to the airport to fly home?

▸ Not being worried about where your child is on a Saturday night?

▸ Not knowing how your son is doing in his freshman history class?

▸ Not having direct access to your child's grades? (Interesting note: once in college, your student's grades are sent to him, not to you.)

▶   Filling your days without chaperoning and chauffeuring responsibilities?

▶   Talking about yourself rather than your kids?

▶   Giving your child her own credit card?

▶   Accepting that your son might live on pizza and ice cream for an entire semester?

The ability to lessen internal and external pressures will help you and your family adapt along the way. Generally, if your family can harmoniously survive the life-cycle stresses of adolescence, then everyone will be happier in the long run.

A key step is to self-examine your parenting style. Explore and reflect on where you fall on the parenting continuum of overprotection versus disengagement. Since the birth of your child, how have you and your spouse handled the job of parenting? Have you set firm boundaries and kept your child on a relatively short leash? Or are you closer to the other end of the spectrum, allowing your child much greater freedom of choice and movement?

Each of us, in our role as a parent, falls somewhere along this continuum. Knowing where you stand can be tremendously useful in helping you move forward with your teenager. In the past, you and your spouse have set certain limits and expectations for what you will and will not permit. Therefore, during the college admissions process, your son or daughter will anticipate your behavior. If you have had a permissive style of parenting, your child will expect you to allow him to make most, if not all, college decisions on his own. Clashes may arise if you now change your position—especially if you announce that the college admissions process is too important for you to do otherwise. On the other hand, if you have held firm control over the years, your child may abdicate all responsibility, expecting you to make crucial decisions for him.

How does one balance letting go but holding on during this period? Let's explore the classic teenager-parent discussion about attending college overseas (not just a semester abroad).

At some point, your child may say that she wants to go to a university far away. It's often unclear at this first pronouncement whether your child is truly interested in European schools or if she is simply trying to test your reaction. Let's look at how two families might handle this situation.

Smith Family

DAUGHTER: "I've decided that I want to go to St. Andrews in Scotland."
DAD: "That's a great idea, as long as you pay for it yourself."
MOM: "Oh, my gosh, you can't go that far away from home. We'll never see you."
DAUGHTER: "You just want to tell me what to do. I've thought this through. Their medieval studies department is exceptional and I want to go."

Mr. Smith becomes more agitated not only because of the cost and distance, but also because he wanted his child to attend a school in the state university system.

Mrs. Smith huffs out of the room, crying, because to her ears her teenager just told her that she doesn't love her any more.

The daughter thinks that while the parents talk about independence, they don't really believe in granting it. As she understands it, mom and dad want her to do what they want her to do.

Later that night, the parents announce that going overseas is simply not an option.

Now let's look at how the neighbors, the Joneses, handled the same announcement.

Jones Family

DAUGHTER: "I've decided that I want to go to St. Andrews in Scotland."
DAD: "Wow, that's really far away. But let's talk about it."
MOM: "We would worry about you being so far away, but what makes the school appealing to you?"
DAUGHTER: "Actually, it has a great medieval studies department, and I could meet students from all over the world there."
DAD: "I had hoped that you would go to one of our excellent state schools, but I understand you're a different person than I am. So we can go ahead and explore."

MOM: "It's not so easy to come home from Scotland for long weekends. But we can explore this possibility—as long as you understand the logistical challenges of this experience, including flights and student visas."

There are dozens of issues that get played out in thousands of similar living-room conversations. This scenario raises issues of money, distance from home, control, family decision making, parents' willingness to let go, trusting your child's judgment, and preconceived expectations.

By considering various aspects of your child's interest in St. Andrews, you are recognizing that adolescence is a time when anything seems possible. Teenagers tend to say out loud whatever hastily conceived ideas they may have. There is no verbal censoring. By demonstrating your willingness to hear your child out, you're modeling caring, respectful behavior. Rather than reacting with horror, being dismissive, or raging at her irrationality, you should simply begin exploring options with her.

Parents often fall into the trap of believing that if they do not immediately quash their child's half-baked ideas, they're encouraging them. It's actually just the opposite. When parents allow their teen to argue his own case, often the teenager recognizes the irrationality of his position. However, by immediately saying no to ideas, you're setting up a conflict situation. You might as well wave a red flag in front of a bull. What teenager can resist a good argument? If you say no, he feels compelled to cling to his position. By remaining seemingly neutral, your child has to take greater personal responsibility for his decision.

Keep in mind that you usually have an ace up your sleeve, which is ultimate veto power. Be careful, though. You don't want to play this card too often or too quickly.

Let's return to your teenager. He will at some point realize that Scotland is considerably more difficult to get to than Pennsylvania or Wisconsin. But let him come to that realization on his own. During the college search, it's quite normal for students to fantasize about faraway adventures. However, as the process proceeds, 99 percent of students begin to think about how they'll get to and from home, how they'll do their laundry, and how they'll be able to stay in touch with their high school friends.

By immediately puncturing your adolescent's fantasy, you may only unleash defiance and rebelliousness. Strategically, it works much better to offer yourself to your child as a sounding board. Feel free to ask questions, in a curious manner, as to why he is thinking of schools abroad. What are the advantages and disadvantages? Suggesting, and then demonstrating, that this is ultimately a family decision but one in which you respect your teenager's position (after all, he's the one going to college) goes a long way toward preventing conflict.

Frequently, families will say to their child, go ahead and explore anywhere. However, they then proceed to set an arbitrary limitation, such as the university must be within a three-hour drive from home or must be east or west of the Mississippi River. From an admissions perspective alone, this is not always a sound idea. There are many good universities that will be outside of these boundaries—many of which might have programs best tailored to your student and some of which might be willing to offer your son or daughter a significant financial aid package.

~The college search usually starts long before students have to make a final selection. Use these high school years to search together, demonstrating the importance of staying connected while respecting the needs of your teenager to move on to greater personal responsibility. ~

From a family perspective, it's healthy for kids to begin to define parameters on their own terms. Encourage your teenager to explore all his options. Try to physically take your student to visit as many campuses as possible. Such visits will help both your child and the whole family understand the impact that his college choices might have on your family. After a few weeks or months, the attention of most teenagers will return to places they know and universities with which they are most familiar.

Ultimately, parents can question a choice of college, and it's certainly within their right to rule out some choices—regardless of emotional reactions. Start thinking about which parameters are really necessary and how to incorporate them into family decision making.

The college search usually starts long before students have to make a final selection. Use these high school years to search together, demonstrating the importance of staying connected while respecting the need of your teenager to move on to greater personal responsibility.

To do so, adolescents need to develop a real sense of self. We know that interpersonal relatedness is the key to developing a sense of who we are—and who we are not. On one hand, if a teenager is not sufficiently differentiated from his parents, emotional maturity cannot occur. Conversely, if a teenager is too separate, this may lead to relationship difficulties. Teenagers like to be independent and loved at the same time. Of course, you as a parent also want to know that your child will accept this independent love—and that you, too, will still be loved.

It's helpful to recognize where you fall on the spectrum of decision making for your child. Families develop different decision-making habits over the years. Some families are more flexible than others, and this has consequences for not only family harmony, but also for positive college admissions outcomes.

Natalie and Rebellion

Natalie was accustomed to having both parents make most major decisions for her. They managed her school course load, directed her after-school activities, and closely monitored her social life. When she turned fifteen, she started asserting herself, demanding a greater say in what she did every day. Her parents were a little shocked by this change and uncomfortable with her challenging their rules. Instead of recognizing the developmental appropriateness of Natalie's behavior, they decided to more closely monitor her actions. This reaction, in turn, began a negative cycle of rebelliousness and punishment. By the time the college admissions process was on the immediate horizon, Natalie and her parents were incapable of calmly and clearly communicating their wants and needs to each other. In this case, instead of working together toward a common goal, they needed to focus on their communication issues with the assistance of a third party—before they could even begin dealing with the college search.

This need manifested itself when Natalie's parents hired an SAT tutor to help improve her scores—without asking her first. When her parents informed her of the impending appointments, Natalie categorically refused to cooperate. The parents' anxiety about ensuring their daughter's success got in the way of their ability to discuss the issue. Not surprisingly, given their history of making decisions for Natalie, they were unable to conceive of a mutual dialogue. Even if this situation feels vaguely familiar to you and your family, there's almost always time to shift gears. In fact, you can use the admissions process as a way to gradually bring your teenager into a decision-making role.

Erica and Decision Making

Erica's parents, on the other hand, were sensitive to the adolescent maturation process. Over the past several years, her parents had been encouraging her decision making when they felt it was safe and appropriate. Erica chose which extracurricular activities to pursue. She decided to drop the varsity tennis team to devote more time to her pursuit of music. She discussed this decision with her parents, and they were able to listen calmly and respectfully. They in fact disagreed with Erica's decision, but they decided that ultimately it was hers to make. First, they offered their arguments, but then were willing to listen to their daughter's arguments. They were respectful of Erica's thought process and decision-making considerations. Later that year, when Erica proposed a summer cross-country sightseeing road trip with a friend, her parents once again listened carefully. This time the parents insisted on security measures that would need to be followed if she truly wanted to take this trip. Because the parents and Erica had already established a mutually respectful relationship, Erica accepted her parents' limitations without argument.

Given the foundation that Erica and her parents had in relating to one another, they were able to discuss viewpoints and negotiate successfully during the college admissions process. There was mutual respect, which let everyone feel that they could be heard while talking things over.

❧

The college search by definition involves choices. Teenagers and parents who already have learned how to talk respectfully about their differences generally have an easier time navigating the college admissions process. Despite their different views, students and parents who have learned to talk and listen respectfully can negotiate and are therefore usually able to identify mutually acceptable college options.

Take stock and evaluate yourself and the roots and wings you are encouraging in your child. Even when you feel comfortable with your teenager's desire for decision-making authority, figuring out where and how to give up control still can be problematic. Reviewing how your family has made decisions in the past and how the decision-making process might—or should—change during the college search is an important next step.

2

Shifts in Family Control

Decisions, decisions, decisions. The college admissions process abounds with them. At each step, parents and students are confronted with a range of academic programs, summer activities, and extracurricular involvement, as well as financial and geographic considerations. To minimize conflict, it's crucial for you to explore and understand who in your family has control over decisions.

Families deal with decision making differently, depending on their personalities, values, and backgrounds. Decision making evolves over time as your child develops. How consensus and decisions are reached about your child will change as you and your family pass through developmental phases. What works with your one-year-old will be different from what works with your eight-year-old, which may be vastly different from what works with your teenager.

When we discuss decision making, we're talking about *control*, the distribution of power, and the roles we each have within the family. The person in control is really the decision maker. Every family is different in terms of who has control and how often the person in control asserts it.

There may be a familial shift in control that occurs during the college admissions process that may affect decision making. A common situation involves working dads who have been on the sidelines for years about child-related decisions but who now demand an active role.

Control can even skip generations. Grandparents come into the picture increasingly, especially if they're paying the tuition bills. They too may want an active role, but their reference points and information about various colleges may be outdated. Ironically, though, many retired grandparents with more free time than the parents are able to get up to speed faster through both campus visits and reading. In such cases, the grandparents learn the present-day admissions realities faster than some parents and prove to be invaluable during key decision-making moments of the college admissions process. This involvement can put some stress on the family, however, as there are now three different generational perspectives to consider.

Older and younger siblings may want to put their two cents into the mix. Older siblings often encourage their younger siblings to go to the same college in order to validate their own position and experience. Sibling rivalry and jockeying for parental attention may also affect decision making. How funds are divided among the children may lead to conflict about control and who makes decisions. Sometimes, there can be conflict between spouses in their roles as alumni, leading to power struggles as to which legacy institution rises to the top of the college list.

It's important to examine who in your family has control, both to understand the history of decision making as well as to figure out how you as a family want to make decisions regarding the college admissions process. Is one parent always in charge? Or do you and your spouse implicitly understand who is in charge of particular areas? Or have you made explicit agreements as to who controls various domains of family life? Perhaps you're at a stage in which you're trying to allow your teenager to make more decisions. She may believe she is in control. Allocating control and responsibility is an evolutionary process for most families, one that accelerates during the high school years.

When it comes to control issues regarding children, there are two basic styles of decision making that can occur within families. Families are not usually at the extreme ends of this continuum; instead they lean in one direction or the other. Parents might be autocratic, evidencing a track record of trying to make all decisions for the children. This style can lead to divisiveness over even early steps, including which colleges should be considered, when and what standardized tests to take, when and where to make college visits, whether or not to apply early decision, and who will fill out the biographical information parts of various applications. Parents may even take over the role of writing college essays.

The other family extreme is the democratic-management style, in which children can make decisions independent of any parental oversight. Parents at this end of the continuum believe they're not entitled to set limits on their children's behavior.

Either of these extremes may lead to conflict and stress if a resolution regarding college decision making is not clearly established early in the process.

Autocratic parents may feel their control slipping away, which can lead to stress and, in some cases, angry shouting matches. Parents who tend to be controlling of their child often do so out of a desire to protect her from harm. Fearing that your child is unable to make good decisions may lead you into a pattern of making important decisions for her. But as your teenager begins to push for more autonomy, this will probably ratchet up the level of disagreement. The more you try to assert the control you had before, the more your teenager pushes back. Given that it's developmentally appropriate for adolescents to begin to assert their independence, and that your child will be the person actually attending college, this assertion of independence is not illogical.

More laissez-faire parents may recognize that, given the enormity of the college choice process, they're no longer willing to totally abdicate decision-making authority. This change in turn may lead to huge arguments with teenagers who are not used to having parents assert control. Instead of a harmonious process, parents and teens may find themselves in a constant state of tension, locked in an emotional standoff.

DIVISION OF CONTROL: WHEN PARENTS DISAGREE

Family members need to feel comfortable with the division of control. If there is a clear acknowledgment that the mother or father is the head of the household and should be responsible for major family decisions, the family may operate quite smoothly. However, if there is an ongoing power struggle among family members, conflict often arises.

The division of labor and control in some families is based upon traditional gender roles. For example, dad works outside the home, pays bills, and mows the lawn while mom takes care of the kids, makes school decisions, and cooks the meals. What happens when mom is the parent who works outside the home? What if there are two moms? Or both parents are employed? If the division-of-labor scenarios are comfortable and accepted by all, the family runs smoothly. If not, families will hit many bumps. When examining your own family, you may recognize when your interactions have run smoothly and when there have been missteps. It's useful to anticipate where your decision making may need to be fine-tuned during this often stressful period.

Do not get caught up in whether your family's decision-making style meets any preconceived notions or fits any so-called norms; instead look at who has control over what and when, and whether it works. Does it get you to what ultimately proves to be the best decision? Is everyone in your family satisfied with the process? Even if it does lead to the best decision, does resentment simmer in the background because someone feels ignored or unfairly burdened?

Not only may you and your teenager disagree about decisions and setting limits, but also you and your spouse may disagree with each other, creating an additional layer of possible conflict and confusion. The college admissions process may touch off long-standing marital issues surrounding conflict resolution, parenting styles, and control. Other potential sources of disagreement include differing values attached to educational goals, status, money, and expectations for children.

> ∼Do not get caught up in whether your family's decision-making style meets any preconceived notions or fits any so-called norms; instead look at who has control over what and when, and whether it works. ∼

So what happens if there's tension between you and your spouse about decision making and control, especially about issues directly related to the preparation for college? Do you find yourself constantly wrangling over the appropriate curfew for your daughter—or what to do when she breaks it—or not agreeing about whether she should take Advanced Placement classes in senior year as well as junior year?

When these conflicts occur, the stress between you and your spouse about who is in charge may be even more dramatic than the parent-child conflict. If there's ongoing parental struggle over who has decision-making authority, your adolescent may openly rebel and act out. Children hate to see parents argue, especially when it has to do with them. Although there may be a temporary positive benefit from split parental decisions (e.g., the child may be off the hot seat about something she has done), in the long run, children are made anxious and tense by parental disagreements. Conflict about control is generally a sign that the college admissions process is not going to be a smooth trip.

Here are some suggestions for reducing such conflict. In order to reach this goal, you need to examine conflicts from different viewpoints. First, you, your spouse, and anyone in your family who is typically involved in decision making should examine the areas of agreement regarding childrearing issues.

Checklist

Do you agree or disagree? Discuss.

- Parents should make all decisions regarding their teenager's curfew.
- Parents should control the allowance and spending habits of their teenager.
- Parents should go with teenagers when teenagers want to purchase major articles of clothing.
- Parents of high school students should receive regular academic performance updates.
- Parents should call other parents to determine the nature of various social gatherings.
- Parents should have the ultimate veto power over college selection.
- Parents should monitor television, cell phone, and computer usage.

Now your family has the beginning of a framework through which you can (1) understand where you agree and disagree, (2) begin to discuss ways to "agree to disagree," and (3) decide who gets to make the final decision if you can't agree.

Maintaining mutually respectful positions can be crucial, even if you don't ultimately agree. You will likely find the process of *trying* to understand each other's positions to be valuable.

Here is a way to help various members of your family understand one another's positions—using the college admissions scenario. Each family member should respond to the following questions:

- What are your expectations for the admissions process?
- What kinds of colleges do you think would be a good fit for your student?
- From your vantage point, are there any non-negotiable decisions (e.g., distance from home, cost, college curriculum)?
- When do you feel parents should make the decisions?
- When do you feel your child should make her own decisions?

You may be pleasantly surprised to find there's a great deal of accord within your family. If not, it's time to work toward reaching greater agreement.

Reaching Agreement

Initially, write down the pros and cons of your positions. Exchange your responses with one another. This will help you assess the advantages and disadvantages of each other's positions. It will feel less emotional because it's in writing, and you will not be compelled to verbally defend yourself.

Stick to the reading/writing scenario at first. If you branch off into discussion and find you're actually listening to one another, give each person the opportunity to amend his or her responses.

If one parent is adamant about their student remaining close to home, but the other parent endorses the option of faraway schools, this exercise will help you understand each other's positions as a first step toward reaching consensus.

Use your active-listening skills. Focus on what the other person is saying. Try to rephrase his thought and then ask if you captured the essence of that thought.

When an issue is too emotional, or when tempers flare, agree to not talk about that issue for a predetermined period of time. Stick to that decision. You can revisit the issue later, when it may feel less emotional. You may find that with the passage of time, you are not wedded to your position as strongly as you thought at first. It also gives you time to absorb and deliberate about each other's positions.

If all else fails, you need to agree on what you will do if you and your spouse can't come to agreement on one or more major points.

One approach is to give your teenager the tie-breaking vote. You need to consider this decision carefully because you will need to be comfortable with the consequences. As an example, you may decide that it's appropriate for your child to cast the tie-breaking vote regarding distance from home but not a cap on the total cost of his education.

An alternative is to consult with a third party who can either help you sort out these issues further or, if you prefer, make a decision for you. A third party can be a grandparent, close family friend, college counselor, or therapist.

~When an issue is too emotional, or when tempers flare, agree to not talk about that issue for a predetermined period of time.~

These exercises can be a good learning experience for your child. Observing one's parents calmly discuss an emotionally charged topic (e.g., how much the family can afford to spend on college tuition or anxiety about future careers) without anger is a potent lesson. Watching this behavior will, in turn, help your child model the same behavior with you.

PARENT-CHILD DISAGREEMENTS

A teenager and his father walk into an admissions office. They take their seats around a big conference room table. An admissions officer gives a short presentation and then asks the student a simple question. The dad, sitting next to his child, not only answers the question but also responds by using the word "we."

Once you and your spouse feel comfortable about the way you can reach agreement regarding admissions decisions, it's time to look at the changing relationship between parents and child.

The last few years of high school are the time when it is appropriate to begin giving your teenager more say in decision making. But this change is a balancing act that each family must go through. Understanding when teenagers should be given more responsibility and when it is appropriate for parents to remain in control is extremely complex.

Over the years, how has money been handled? If your teenager has had a job, did he have control over spending or saving, or did you? Was there a great deal of negotiating and arguing before a decision was reached, or was the process relatively painless and acceptable to everyone?

Consider driving privileges. Does your teenager own his own car? What, if any, restrictions have you placed on driving? The car not only represents independence and autonomy for your son or daughter, it literally gives him or her freedom to separate from home. Allowing your teenager to drive unchaperoned is often the ultimate manifestation of trust.

Regardless of the source of conflict over control in your family, we want you to bypass adolescent rebellion issues as much as possible when dealing with the college search. Avoid having this process become a source of conflict and power struggles. Rather, seize the chance to enhance communication in your family. Not only will a conflict-laden college search probably lead to poor choices, but it also has the potential to permanently color family relationships just as your child is preparing to leave the nest.

To smooth the process of allowing your teenager a greater role in appropriate decision-making tasks, try these exercises. Your answers may shed light on some problems with your present control patterns and help you shift control more comfortably and rationally.

Exercise 1: Keys to the Kingdom

Make a list of five decisions that will need to be made in the next month—decisions that you're comfortable allowing your teenager to make on his own. Two or three of these decisions should relate to college applications.

Then make a list of five decisions that will need to be made in the next month—decisions that you are not comfortable letting your teenager make on his own.

Share these two lists with your student and practice active listening. See how well you can reach a consensus on what your teenager can decide, what you may need to decide, and what you need to decide together.

Exercise 2: Hands-Off, Hands-On

Give your child a simple and early college admissions task such as doing an Internet search or requesting college catalogs. Notice how comfortable you are with your child's performance of this task. Your job here is simply to be an observer.

▶ Did she complete the task within your time expectations? How long did you think it would take her?

▶ How long before you had the desire to nag?

▶ Were you able to maintain a hands-off policy?

When the task is completed, you and your teenager should have a debriefing to see how each of you felt about the process and to explore constructive ideas for future division of control.

TEACHING YOUR CHILD HOW TO MAKE DECISIONS

Overall, there needs to be some give and take as you and your student discover the appropriate balance of control in your family. As a follow-up to the Internet search exercise, ask your daughter to come up with a list of twenty colleges—without setting any initial parameters.

The results will likely help you see your child's perspectives about the college admissions process, her views about her academic achievements, and her aspirations for the future.

Understanding her present level of investment in the college search will help you decide how to proceed with dividing up college-related decision making. For example, you might be comfortable giving an eager beaver more leeway in planning a college visit than you would give someone who is reluctant.

As we've said, there may be some tension regarding distance from home or finances. Be somewhat flexible at this point. If you or your spouse previously considered a maximum of a five-hour drive, let your student explore universities within a five-hour flight. This flexibility is not necessarily abdicating parental control. Rather, you are allowing your teenager to test her ideas in a safe way. You are not agreeing to anything at this point. You are just encouraging her to explore and think for herself.

Decision making does not come naturally to teenagers. Often they want to first consult with their peers, or they want to be clear they are choosing something different from what you want. Teenagers' egos also are fragile. They do not want to risk making a bad decision, so they conclude that avoidance is safer.

Asking your child to make simple decisions, even about benign topics such as the color of clothes or food selection, can lead to "I don't know." This apparent indifference does not mean, however, that she wants anyone else making decisions for her—especially parents.

This presents a double bind for parents. You offer to allow your student to make a decision for herself, but she avoids doing so. You offer to step in to make the decision for her, but then she becomes angry that you are treating her like a baby. The best approach is to discuss this predicament directly.

Describe the scenario and ask for her solution. If you tell her that she can call up admissions offices to plan an interview, but she fails to do so, what should you do? We suggest you give your teenager a choice—either she must step up and take responsibility, or you will do it for her. Use this general strategy with your teenager when you find yourself stuck between your student's passivity and her defensiveness.

Often parents can use the college admissions process to help hone their teenagers' confidence and decision-making skills. Students learn to weigh the pros and cons of their choices. Do they want to be close to home or not? Would they like a big or a small school? Coed or single sex? Having family discussions in which you encourage your child to express her opinion and explore various options can provide invaluable practice.

Some of the decisions that students can make early in their high school careers involve extracurricular activities. Let your child determine if she wants to put in the time and effort to make the soccer team or perform in the school play.

A general rule: when helping people with decision making, it's a good idea to couch decisions as options. Begin by giving your student choices. She can play soccer or be in the play, but she has to choose one of them. You also can teach decision making with timelines. For example, your teenager can register for a standardized test right now while you're available to help or by next week on her own. Again, she needs to choose—and in a timely fashion.

When you allow your student to make decisions, you need to be comfortable with her making a bad decision. Establish consequences for procrastination. If your child doesn't register for the SAT or ACT, you will need to register for her, and you will probably need to revoke some of her decision-making privileges.

The college application process can lead your teenager to feel more comfortable allowing others to be involved in decision making. Teenagers can learn to value input from other people, including teachers, guidance counselors, alumni, relatives, and coaches. Teenagers value the thoughts of those they respect. Students may appreciate hearing a nonparental adult's perspective on their strengths and weaknesses. Such adults may recognize traits about your teenager that neither you nor she were aware of. Moreover, professionals in her field of interest might be able to share with her what other people have done to become successful.

FEAR OF LOSING CONTROL

The college admissions process elicits feelings of loss of control for parents and teenagers alike. Your adolescent has to apply to schools that she is interested in attending, but other, unknown people will ultimately make the decision as to whether she is admitted. This is inherently stressful for students, but in our experience it's almost as stressful, if not more so, for parents.

During the application process, many parents begin to reflect on their seventeen years of childrearing and cannot help but feel they will be judged for their years of effort. It's also scary and sometimes hurtful to have other people judge your child. As a parent, you feel inherently entitled to critique your own child and to complain about her bad habits, procrastination, lack of effort, or indifference. But if someone else does so—especially when that someone is a nameless, faceless admissions committee—it can trigger powerful emotions, including anger, pain, embarrassment, and defensiveness.

By sending in an application, your child, and you by default, agree to allow someone else to judge her in the first place. This understanding may not fully ease the tension over having others judge your child, but it does provide a sense of control. The more comfortable you are with the fact that admissions committees have the ultimate decision-making authority, the more comfortable you are likely to feel about the entire process. Sometimes it's empowering to just go with the process and depersonalize the issue of selection.

Being able to discuss difficult issues comfortably with all family members helps reduce stress and anxiety tremendously. Talking about the limitations of control that play out during the admissions process may serve to allay many concerns. You and your family can list all the things over which you do have control: schools you choose to visit, test preparation courses, extracurricular activities, essay topics to write about, and the financial resources you plan to use for college. Most important, you and your child have control of where your student decides to apply.

~The college admissions process elicits feelings of loss of control for parents and teenagers alike. Your adolescent has to apply to schools that she is interested in attending, but other, unknown people will ultimately make the decision as to whether she is admitted.~

Control on a Daily Basis

There are many areas of daily life over which you and your teenager do not have control: the weather, your boss's mood, her teacher's mood, and how the other members of her basketball team are playing that day. You can each talk about how it makes you feel when you do have some control over situations and when you don't. Share how you may each deal with lack of control. Does it make you angry? Frustrated? Depressed? Are you able to shrug it off easily? Do you blame yourself?

A common consequence of feeling out of control is to literally become depressed. Clinically depressed people often have difficulty recognizing where they do have choices and options, as they may be experiencing a profound loss of control in their lives. It is important to put the college application process in perspective. Yes, it's stressful and creates tension and anxiety. You have to begin ceding some areas of control to your teenager, and you both have to relinquish control to college admissions officers. But it can also be an exciting adventure. You can look upon the experience as a life lesson in how to be more comfortable with having less control.

It can be helpful to play worst-case scenario games. Ask one another what is the worst thing that could happen during the college admissions process. Is the worst not getting into the college of one's choice? Is it not getting in anywhere at all or not receiving any financial aid? Imagine how you would deal with these situations, trying to envision the disappointment—then recognize that students can almost always find some college to attend.

Looking at the worst possible outcome can make it easier to let go of your fear. You can be freed up to focus on trying to achieve your goals, rather than worrying about not achieving them.

Now is a perfect time to reinforce all the wonderful attributes of your teenager. Discuss her strengths and good qualities. Underscore that even if an admissions committee fails to accept her, it's not a reflection of her inherent goodness. Plenty of people enjoy soccer, even though they know they won't play in the next World Cup. Thousands sing in school musicals, even though they know they won't perform on Broadway. Countless more study economics, even though it is unlikely that they will ever serve on the Federal Reserve Board. Millions of people lead happy, fulfilling lives without ever having gone to Harvard, becoming a senator, or earning enough money to buy their own airplane.

While remaining aware of the constraints of the college admissions process, you should make sure each family member is able to take a break from the stress. This is an opportunity for families to enjoy time together and develop a repertoire of pleasurable activities. Think about the things that you enjoy doing: Seeing movies? Reading? Playing sports? Listening to music? Learn to reinforce yourself and other family members when you are feeling down or not in control.

Use each other as a support system. Talk to friends and other families who are going through the admissions process. Try to find the humor in some of the situations, and try to put the process into perspective. Without minimizing the importance of college selection, it's not the final determinant of a person's life course. Work together on taking the task seriously but also on being able to step away when it feels overwhelming. Life is filled with situations that we cannot control, so we all can benefit from developing the skills necessary to tolerate these situations without becoming crushed by them.

How to Regain Control

How do you re-establish a decision-making role if you have already relinquished a great deal of control?

This type of situation often occurs when a teenager has maintained her own schedule for some time and pretty much comes and goes as she pleases. Then, say, at the beginning of tenth grade, her parents announce that she needs to start looking at colleges and that the entire family, therefore, needs to monitor her schedule.

From your teenager's perspective, you already gave up control, and she's not eager to give it back. You, on the other hand, need to be comfortable reasserting your decision-making authority. It doesn't have to be an all-or-nothing proposition. Your student can continue making many decisions that affect her daily life. Your task is to outline those critical decisions about her educational future that are now going to involve the family. Share with your teenager this limited list of when you need to have a say in the decision-making process. This usually includes money, visiting colleges, and deadlines.

One way in which you retain control is that your teenager still lives in your house. Presumably you still provide her with food, if not spending money and chauffeur services. You have a say in transportation, household chores, and use of family living spaces. You also have the power of the purse, unless your child is working and has complete control over her wages.

Unfortunately, you already may have lost control over personal hygiene and the cleanliness of your teenager's room. One of the most predictable—and humorous—discussions we have every year with families takes place just before college interviews. Parents call us in exasperation after their child asks if it's okay to wear a nice T-shirt to a college interview. You still are the parent, and you have the right to expect certain behaviors when your child is in your home.

Many families begin negotiations about their child's social network and Internet and cell phone usage. Often parents grant greater privileges based upon the actions of the teenager. For example, if your student is doing well in school and is taking care of her home obligations, she will be allowed more privileges—such as use of the car. However, if your student is not acting responsibly about those issues that you believe are critical, like her school performance, then it's certainly within your rights to rein in her behavior with more household chores and fewer social activities.

A key parenting strategy is knowing when to pick your battles. When should I give up control, and when should I retain it? One example may concern your child's selection of clothes. Can you allow your teenager to wear what she wants? Where do you draw the line? Do you facilitate her clothes selection by paying for whatever she chooses? Or do you give her the responsibility of selecting, and also purchasing, her own wardrobe? Do you allow her to wear whatever she wants to school but not when she is going out with the family or to a college interview?

Answering these questions will help you determine the battles worth fighting for in the college admissions process. You may come to realize that your child's wanting to attend college in a warm climate is not worth an all-out war. On the other hand, decisions that involve $200,000 are not appropriate to automatically cede.

If you relinquish control of the college admissions process too quickly, you may initially avoid having to deal with conflict, but you may leave your student floundering. Most teenagers do not have all the resources or ability to broadly explore colleges and college options. Without careful guidance, children may over- or underestimate their college admissibility. Your child might be focusing on minor issues, such as whether or not a college has certain exercise equipment, rather than on academic departments and job placement afterward—not to mention the overall fit of the university.

3

Peer and Social Pressure

Peers play a powerful role in the life of a teen. It's normal for adolescents to become more and more focused on what their friends think and do. Teenagers are often consumed with anxiety about their position in their school's social hierarchy. You, as the parent, may feel your influence slipping away. Your opinions seem to become less important or reasonable, according to your child. Nonetheless, you still have a great deal of authority and control.

During high school—and especially during the college admissions process—your student will challenge your ideas, values, and limits. Often you may feel that you're in an active tug-of-war with your child's peers over her welfare and future.

You may struggle to establish limits with your teen that are often in stark contrast to the values of her peer group. You may have already engaged in these battles, but the stakes become even higher when college is the issue. Planning for college starts earlier than it did even five years ago. Mapping out your child's high school career, both her academic course load as well as extracurricular and summer activities, often begins before ninth grade.

~An additional consideration is your own experience of peer pressure. Just because we are adults does not mean we are immune to the influence of our peers.~

An additional consideration is your own experience of peer pressure. Just because we are adults does not mean we are immune to the influence of our peers. How much we are each influenced by our friends and social network varies. But peers are a potentially powerful influence for each person in the family. It's vital to explore how much our thinking is influenced by those around us.

COMPARISONS, COMPARISONS, COMPARISONS

Your child has undoubtedly already shown signs of this growing preoccupation with his peer group. Often it starts benignly with comparisons to other children and their families. "Mom, why can't I go to the concert on Saturday? Everybody who's anybody will be there!" Or, "Dad, please let me stay out until 2 a.m. No one else's parents make them come home at midnight." Teenagers try to use these comparisons as leverage to get the results they want (e.g., to have a later curfew, be allowed to participate in more mature activities, or have more responsibility). Equally important, though, is your child's feeling that he does not want to be different.

How did this play out in the home of forty-five-year-old Barbara, mother of teenager Beth? Barbara shares a story about her daughter that underscores the pull that your teenager often experiences, between doing what her peer group wants and following your lead (or even her own).

Beth, who had recently acquired her driver's license, announced to her mother that she had offered to drive a number of her friends to a rock concert about forty miles away. The mother told her daughter she would not be allowed to borrow the car to do so, and she would have to tell her friends to make other arrangements. The daughter proceeded to throw an enormous tantrum, announcing that her life was over, her friends would never speak to her again, and she could not show her face in school because of her humiliation. Barbara held her ground, and eventually the girlfriends made other plans.

Several months later, her daughter slipped into a conversation that she was actually thankful that her mother had forbidden her from driving to the concert. She had felt terribly nervous about having to drive, but she was afraid to reveal her feelings to her friends for fear of being ridiculed. Her mother had given her a graceful way to save face ("Blame it on my mom.").

It is a rare child who actually returns to his parents and overtly thanks them for setting limits. Still, your efforts will be appreciated.

Adolescents compete on all playing fields, literally and figuratively. Girls are often consumed with concerns about their looks. Are they pretty enough? Skinny enough? Are their clothes hip enough? The pressure to conform is enormous, which accounts for the rampant increase in the number of cases of eating disorders—now not just limited to females. Boys want to be seen as cool, too. Are they athletic enough? Do they have all the latest technology? Do they have their own car? How much freedom do parents allow them? Do they have a girlfriend? Is it considered the social norm in your teenager's peer group to drink? How much? By trying to get a handle on your child's social pressures, you'll be helping him cope with multiple concerns, as well as enabling him to focus more clearly on the college admissions process.

Understanding that foremost in your teenager's mind is his concern about what his peers think will give you a tremendous advantage in dealing with him. You can begin to assess where his behavior originates and what pressures are upon him. Wanting to be accepted by peers is a perfectly appropriate desire and is essential to your child's self-esteem. Most adolescents have relatively fragile egos, and they are constantly examining their social status. Skillful handling of these peer stresses is crucial to maintaining stability and a measured course for your student.

~Most adolescents have relatively fragile egos, and they are constantly examining their social status. Skillful handling of these peer stresses is crucial to maintaining stability and a measured course for your student.~

Cell phones, instant messaging, and blogging have intensified the teenage craving to be in the loop. Anxiety abounds if your student is not in constant communication with friends. Something critical might happen without him, which in turn may lead to ostracism or, minimally, lack of inclusion. Will he miss a get-together at someone's house? Will he miss a piece of gossip about someone? Will a friend seek out someone else to confide in or socialize with because he was unavailable?

Millions of families struggle with how to manage their children's passionate need to be in constant touch with peers. Children as young as seven or eight are already demanding unlimited computer access so they can maintain 24/7 contact. Cell phone companies are marketing phones to preteens. As a parent of a teenager, you know firsthand how much energy can be consumed in debating teenage pressure to maintain contact and status within a group of friends. How do you handle the barrage of comparisons to other teens and their parents?

Questions to Ask About Your Child's Peer Relationships:

▶ Has your child ever gotten into trouble at school because he was "just following along" with his friends?

▶ Does your child wear the latest designer labels or does he prefer to shop independently of his peers?

▶ Does your child tend to participate in group activities, at school or after school, or does he prefer to engage in more solitary activities?

▶ Does your child generally seek out leadership opportunities?

▶ Historically, does your child tend to be teased? Or to be the teaser?

▶ When your child sees some form of injustice, including bullying, does he stand up for others?

A related issue to the importance of peer relationships is your comfort level with your child's friends. If you're happy with his social group and feel they are a positive influence, life is much simpler for you. However, how do you handle the situation when you feel your son or daughter is being influenced by adolescents whose judgment you find lacking?

Many teenagers are reluctant to work to their full potential if no one else in their group does. If the peer group norm in your community is to go home from school and watch television, your teenager will need your emotional support to buck this trend. Articulate to your teenager that you understand that he's in a difficult position; tell him that you recognize that he is struggling to balance wanting to be liked by his peers with needing to be different. It might help to sit down and discuss some options with him. For example, he could watch TV with his friends on Friday night, but engage in academic pursuits during the week.

If all your son's peers are on a sports team, but your son is just not athletic, once again your support is crucial. Encourage him to engage in activities that he enjoys, not those prescribed by his friends. Be enthusiastic about your child's chosen activity, whatever his choice might be. For instance, if your son prefers singing in the school chorus, you can demonstrate your support, not only by attending all his concerts, but perhaps even rehearsals as well. When talking with his friends and their parents, you can share your enthusiasm for his interests.

Your teenager's peer group may not offer "permission" to be different, so it is your job to be supportive when he is. If your student is going to be overwhelmed by taking too many Advanced Placement classes, yet he's afraid to admit this to his peer group, perhaps you should step in and suggest he lower his academic pressure.

On the other hand, if your child's friends look upon students who do well in school as geeks and nerds, you may need to intervene and insist that your student maintain his academic course load. Even though your teenager may argue that none of his friends study as much, work as hard, or take such demanding courses, you may use your parental leverage to ensure that he works in keeping with his abilities.

WHAT DO I NEED TO KNOW ABOUT MYSELF, AS A PARENT?

As parents, we may feel pressure from peers that our children attend a "good" or even "great" college or university. This raises other issues. Will my child live away from home? How much money is available for higher education? What will I tell my friends if she doesn't get into a well-known college? While these are legitimate questions for every family to ask, you should make choices based on your particular family situation. Focusing on the attitudes and interests of our adult peers will intensify the stress and will exacerbate tension between family members. Assess the needs and wishes of each member of your own family, rather than those of the families in your community.

Self-Assessment: Parent Peer Pressure

We urge you to explore how much you, as an adult, fall prey to peer pressure. Ask yourself the following questions and try to answer as candidly as possible. You're the only one who will know these responses, so be honest!

▶ How much do you believe that peer pressure will influence your recommendations to your child during the college search stage?

▶ On a scale of 1-10, how much do you find yourself caring about what other people think? (1=not much at all; 10=a great deal)

▶ How will you feel if a neighbor questions why your child is not applying to any Ivy League schools, especially if you know that her child will be? And how will you feel if the reason relates to your child's lower academic achievements?

▶ How will you feel if your peers all give you a blank stare when you share with them the unfamiliar names of a number of colleges that your child is thinking about applying to?

▶ How will you feel if your peers all give you an envious look when you tell them that your daughter is considering applying to Brown?

▶ How will you feel if your child and his college plans are being overlooked by your peers? For instance, if your child is not in the top 10 percent of his class, others may express less interest in his college choices. Will that distress you?

If you would feel uncomfortable in any of the situations described in these questions, would you be able to keep these emotions from your child? We recognize it's difficult to avoid these possible situations with your peers. Our goal is to help you recognize these emotional minefields, not only to protect yourself, but also to avoid having these feelings negatively affect your child.

We realize that it's difficult to immunize yourself against extraneous input. However, you really ought to try. Remember the advice that you gave your child when he was ten years old: just because everyone else is teasing the substitute teacher doesn't mean that he should. You might have given your child some suggestions about alternative responses, such as excusing himself or busying himself with something else. This is a perfect time to reemploy these tried and true techniques.

PEER PRESSURE SPECIFICALLY APPLIED TO THE COLLEGE ADMISSIONS PROCESS

Adolescence is a period of constant self-doubt and self-evaluation. As we have noted, teenagers often obsessively compare themselves to others, wondering if they're good enough. This concern gets plenty of play during the admissions process.

Your child will even experience pressure from her peers as to how to evaluate the college admissions process itself. This pressure can take a number of forms, including rampant competition and denial of the need to plan.

During the college search, both you and your student may feel the strain of peer pressure. Your child may be under significant pressure from her peers regarding when, where, how, and with whom she might be going to college. Additional competitive pressures can arise as peers compare grades, quality of schools, letters of recommendation, who got which summer internship, and so on. The number of college visits, the number of schools applied to, and what schools you can afford will likely create significant pressures on both of you.

The pressure to attend a good private school or the best state school will, of course, vary from locale to locale, but there's almost always some underlying competitive issue. Even the question of whether or not your student will be attending college immediately after high school can add stress.

If the norm for your geographic area is for most high school graduates to attend local or community colleges, families who plan to have their teenager go away to a four-year college often face an emotional uphill battle when exploring these other options. This issue can split families, with one member reinforcing the community norm of staying nearby while one or more members may feel more adventurous.

One Florida family's experience highlights the difficulties that can occur when parents, themselves, disagree. Parents of a bright, talented daughter almost came to blows over their individual wishes for her college years. The mother was insistent on the daughter attending a college within a 100-mile radius. The father, on the other hand, was more interested in making sure the daughter would have a first-rate education and be positioned for top-flight jobs after graduation. Geographically, both could not exist at the same time. The parents simply needed to resolve this issue before their daughter could even begin the search process.

The way the family resolved this was that each parent was able to suggest a short list of colleges, with neither parent having veto power. This enabled the admissions process to proceed and deferred the ultimate school choice question for many months. This time proved to be crucial because the student was not admitted to some of the big-name schools preferred by her father. But her father at least felt that they had tried.

A different scenario involved a Delaware student who went to a large state university because the school's basketball team had performed well at the NCAA tournament the year before. He and his friends had been enthusiastic fans of the team, and many were elated by the prospect of attending that school. Nothing could dissuade this particular student from his decision to attend the large university with many large lecture classes. Even though the university was an excellent educational institution, it was not the ideal place for this young man, who would have been better served by a smaller, hands-on college.

You probably already understand the pressures your child is under, even if you have not yet articulated them. Your teenager may be too proud to discuss his concerns with you directly. As a parent, you can raise the issue. We encourage you to share your own feelings about the pressures you're experiencing during the college search process. Show that you can empathize with what you assume your child is experiencing.

Often students engage in denial to avoid the stress of peer pressure. For example, if you ask your child where his friends are considering applying to college, he may respond that he has no clue. It's possible that this merely reflects the social norm not to discuss this topic among themselves. It may also reflect your son's unwillingness to engage in a conversation about a possibly competitive situation vis-à-vis his friends. Or, it may just reflect your child's desire to avoid the process as much as possible. This response does not necessarily mean that your student is not thinking about and planning for the admissions process. He may choose to keep it within the family rather than drawing his peers into the mix.

The socioeconomic status of your child's peers may influence the college selection process. If you live in an affluent community in which finances are not considered an issue, your child may expect that money does not enter into the college equation. On the other hand, if your child's peers are all limited in their college selection by financial constraints, and you are not, this situation too may create a challenge for you and your teenager.

We advise you to be frank with your teenager about the financial aspects of college. Acknowledge that money may have a direct bearing on college selection. Your student probably is well aware by the time he is in high school of the high cost of college and that some schools are much more expensive than others. We specifically advise you to have detailed discussions about college finances later in the process. In the meantime, we suggest that you begin general discussions about costs and possible sacrifices.

Generally, peers can influence your child in one of two directions. His peers may be fiercely competitive and driven to succeed. The bar is raised to a point where nothing less than admission to a highly selective college will be acceptable. These peers will discuss and plan admissions strategies, often for years, and have their high school years consumed with the goal of admission to college. Even though you may feel your child can benefit from this pressure to perform well and achieve, the emotional toll it takes can be enormous. Can your child keep up with these other students? Does he have the aptitude to achieve at such a high level? Does he truly have the same goals and aspirations? Are your values about college education the same as those of his peers?

Just because peers set up the expectations for success does not mean everyone can achieve at the same level. Be aware of how your student is handling this kind of peer pressure. Is he really up to the demands of a highly rigorous high school curriculum? Or is he just getting by in order to look good to his peers?

Note the following landmarks:

- How is your student doing academically in his more challenging courses, such as calculus?
- Is your student struggling in classes that require a large volume of reading?
- Is your student struggling in classes that require a great deal of writing?
- Even if your student is getting top grades in his classes, how much effort and energy is required to maintain these grades?
- Is your student deriving satisfaction from his academic performance, even though it may be a struggle?

Answering these questions can help parents figure out whether they should continue to encourage the more challenging academic path, or if it's ultimately in the student's best interest to pursue a more comfortable academic track.

The other extreme of peer influence arises from those teenagers who set the norm of not caring about what occurs after high school graduation. There may be the expectation that, of course, college is in the future. Yet, how that will happen, and where one will go, is of little interest. Often these students wait until parents or guidance counselors begin to apply some pressure to make decisions about college applications. Their focus on the present precludes any real interest in planning for the future. This attitude often reinforces the notion that high school is of no value; therefore, it doesn't matter how well you perform. Peers who express these views will often make it difficult for your child to focus on setting higher goals for college admissions.

SUCCESSFUL STRATEGIES AND RESOLUTIONS

The most successful strategy for parents and children is to openly discuss the peer pressure that your student experiences. Conversations are often best held over the dinner table or while driving to an activity, when tempers are cool and people are feeling comfortable and relaxed. You should maintain an active interest in what your teenager's friends are doing. Your child initially may be reluctant to share information, but the key is to ask questions in a nonthreatening manner. For example, asking who is in your child's English class may give you insight into whether your child's peers are going through the same academic experience with him or not. Soliciting information in a curious rather than an accusatorial way may lead to greater insights into your teenager's life.

Begin discussing how your child's peers are addressing the issue of college. How does your student view his friends' interest in the college admissions process? Are his friends motivated and interested? What, if anything, are they doing to prepare? Your child may not be especially forthcoming with this information. As we noted before, he may have one or more reasons for not wishing to engage in a conversation about what his friends are, or are not, doing.

There is a danger in your student being paralyzed by too much input from others. It's generally a good idea to entrust the progress of this process to one knowledgeable professional who can help keep you and your child on track. Avoid, if you can, coffee shop gatherings in which parents compare notes about the progress of their children in the admissions process. Ultimately, these conversations may only serve to raise your anxiety level while simultaneously failing to offer you any reliable information.

You can depend too much on school or your child's peers to get your child to do what you want. For example, parents often mistakenly rely on some school counselors to sign their child up for sufficiently challenging courses. Most school counselors can provide general information about courses or the SAT, but you, yourself, ought to make sure that your son or daughter registers for the most appropriate courses and standardized tests.

There is sometimes the expectation that parents can avoid confrontations with their child by passing off some responsibility to the student's peers. This can be problematic on many fronts, most significantly in relying on youngsters to always do the right and wise thing. If you wait for your teenager to make the first moves, you may be setting him up for failure. If you wait for his peers to pressure him into becoming more proactive in the college admissions process, you and he may lose valuable time and miss opportunities. Not only will your teenager be at a disadvantage strategically regarding his college options, but it will also set up a potentially enormous conflict between the two of you, fueled by frustration and anger. We recommend that you and your child plot your own admissions course, relying on professional input rather than on peers.

One mother was so convinced that her son was on track that she didn't even volunteer to drive him to various campuses to look at schools. She believed, erroneously, that because his friends were visiting many of the same colleges her son was interested in, he was discussing, in depth, what his friends had learned. By the time the mother realized these substantive conversations had not taken place, the family had lost six months that could have been used productively.

A key conversation you should have with your teenager involves mini-

~There is sometimes the expectation that parents can avoid confrontations with their child by passing off some responsibility to the student's peers.~

mizing conflict with your child's peers about the college search process. If your child's friends are not planning to attend a competitive school but your child is, you may encourage him not to bring up college visits with his friends. There's no need to get in the face of his friends about differences regarding their post high school lives.

It's often a good strategy to discuss your own experiences. For example, if you've had to deal with not offending a friend or colleague, you may want to share this with your teenager. On the other hand, it is rarely a good idea to tell your teenager what he should or must do about a situation. Let him reach his own conclusions after hearing what you have to say.

If your child is able to express his dismay about his peer group's obsessive conversations about college, you can suggest he gently tell his friends he doesn't want to talk about it. You may recall earlier conversations you have had with your child about other concerns, such as grades. If the environment of your child's school promotes grade comparison, you may have told your child that it's appropriate to avoid giving information about grades to friends. Whether or not your child did well, he has the option to decline to share his grades. Humor is always a good strategy, as is changing the subject. When asked about his grades, he can reply he did well, thank you very much. If pressed, he can joke that his grades are classified information.

Another strategy for minimizing the negative effects of peer pressure is to discuss your child's goals for the future. In a calm setting, your teenager will probably recognize that he and his friends may move apart, even if at the moment it feels like they are joined at the hip for life. Taking friends out of the mix may allow him to assess his own goals with less distraction.

YOUR TEENAGER'S OBJECTIVES

When your child was young, you probably talked about what she wanted to do when she grew up. Somehow, those conversations tend to get lost in the college search process. A positive family activity is to raise those dreams and aspirations again. You can discuss what your child may envision after college: What kind of job do you want? How might you pursue your passions in a way that you can also make a living? Do you think you will need to get a graduate degree in order to accomplish your career objectives? Where do you imagine you will be in ten years? Twenty years?

Help your student try to view her situation from a different perspective. If your daughter's best friend has a learning disability, discuss how the friend may be exploring her college options. How will she evaluate a college in terms of how it will best suit her needs? After exploring how friends go about making these decisions, the recognition that it has to be a case-by-case decision may help your teenager feel less tied to what others are doing.

Often the focus of concern is the option of staying close to home, maybe even living at home, versus going relatively far away. Your son or daughter may feel pressured in one of these directions. Either it becomes the norm to go far away, or "everyone" is staying close to home. Yet, what is most important is a realistic assessment of what your teenager wants and needs. Your teenager may blame you for pushing her to either stay close to home (if most friends are going far away) or to be more adventurous (if most friends are going to local colleges).

More than 80 percent of students who choose to stay at home for college do so for financial reasons. If this is a primary concern for your family, then discuss this up front. Of course, your daughter will not be able to share in the dorm experience like her friends who reside on campus, but talking honestly about this will likely lessen the blow. Conversely, not every dorm resident has a meaningful campus living experience. Many students come back from their dorms during Thanksgiving convinced that they need to switch roommates because of the high level of conflict.

Give yourself permission to feel some stress, but be aware that your anxiety can contribute to your teenager's pressure. She may always want to please mom and dad, and therefore she will be very sensitive to your feelings. As a family, you need to discuss and clarify your wants and desires. This offers an opportunity to differentiate between what you want for your child and what she truly wants for herself.

In your role as the parent, you can discuss strategies that allow your teenager to go along with certain peer demands and expectations (e.g., buying jeans with a certain name brand) while then helping her to be different in other respects (taking different courses, applying to various colleges). It's unrealistic to expect your student to totally ignore what her friends are doing. Your job is to guide your teenager to understand when it's safe and acceptable to go along with the group and when she needs to forge her own path.

Ted and Peer Pressure

Let's look at how Ted and his family dealt with college-related peer pressure. Ted went to an academic suburban high school and was a top student. He was an Eagle Scout and very much enjoyed hiking and camping. At the start of the admissions process, he and his friends began talking about colleges in Boston, New York, and Los Angeles. The recurring theme that kept coming up was that their home town was boring and that they needed the excitement of a college in a big city.

Ted didn't want to seem uncool, but deep down he really wanted to go to college in a place where he could enjoy the outdoors on a regular basis. He mentioned this once to his friends, who proceeded to tease him about cow tipping. He never brought the issue up again with his friends.

Fortunately, he did discuss his interest in the outdoors with his parents, who encouraged him to look at schools in New Hampshire and Maine. The story had a happy ending with Ted attending Bowdoin College, in Maine, but this situation could have turned out differently if his parents had not had the wisdom and strength to help their son buck their town's existing peer pressure.

What should you do if it appears that your son is about to succumb to peer pressure? In this case, what if Ted announces he wants to apply only to urban schools like his friends, rather than to schools that you, as his parent, know would be a much better fit? You must have a gentle but firm conversation with him, reminding him of the importance of his own interests and talents. You are the voice of experience regarding your child and have the perspective on his short-term versus long-term gratification.

> ∼Give yourself permission to feel some stress, but be aware that your anxiety can contribute to your teenager's pressure.∼

If your child seems stuck for the moment on making choices generated by his peers, the other strategy for you is to insist that your student cast as wide a net as possible. This way, you don't engage in a head-to-head conflict early in the admissions process. Keeping an open mind about various colleges allows you time to work with your teenager to demonstrate how certain schools might be a good fit for him.

Sophie and Parent Pressure

Parent-generated peer pressure also can affect school choice. Sophie's father went to Columbia and for as long as she could remember, her dad and his college friends had been talking about Columbia and what it meant to their lives. At first, Sophie was bored with all these Columbia stories. But after two visits to the campus, she was sold on what a great place Columbia would be for her. The only problem was that she was not a particularly academic student. Believing that she was destined to go to Columbia, she neglected to put much energy or time into her other college applications. She learned that this was not a good decision when she received five college rejections, including one from Columbia.

Sophie's predicament could have been avoided. Encourage your child to apply to her dream school, but advise her not to put all her eggs in one basket. Explain that there may be dozens of schools that will allow your child to achieve what she wants.

The key here is to understand that both you and your child will face peer pressure that can have a powerful impact on the college search. Try to look at the pressures that affect you—as a parent, spouse, neighbor, employee, employer, or community leader. Then help your child understand the pressures that affect her in daily life.

When grappling with pressure from peers, whether from teenagers or adults, the goal is to understand where the expectations are coming from, to assess their value, and to reach an independent conclusion about what works best for your teenager and your family.

4

Objectively Assessing Your Child

The college admissions process may be the first time your child's future is significantly affected by the evaluation of others. Unless your student attended an independent or magnet school that had selective admissions, your family probably avoided situations in which she was assessed in this stringent a manner. Throughout the years, she may have tried out for sports teams, competed in debate tournaments, or entered spelling bees. How your child reacted to these competitive situations may tell you a great deal about how she will likely handle the upcoming process.

Some teenagers actually rise to the occasion and relish this type of competition. Others abhor competitive situations, doing whatever they can to avoid them. These are children who refused to take music lessons, partly to avoid having to perform in a recital, or who chose not to join any competitive team, from swimming to gymnastics. Neither personality type is better than the other. But knowing your child's feelings about competition is important to understanding how she will handle being evaluated by others.

The college application process intensifies competition since the emphasis allegedly is on evaluating the whole person, and not necessarily one specific talent. The prospect of a college admissions committee examining all facets of your child's development can be daunting. It's stressful enough to try out for ballet school or the wrestling team, but a multifaceted appraisal by a college admissions officer can be downright nerve-wracking.

Each of us has a notion of where we stand in the world and how we stack up in specific arenas—how good we look compared to others, how successful we are, how happy we are, or how well we have raised our children. We can define our success in any way we want. For example, we may feel successful because we make a lot of money. Or we may value success by working at something we really enjoy, even if it does not pay well.

We also all have our own measures of how we evaluate our children. Some of us use academic performance, or athletic prowess, or politeness. Even if you pride yourself on being objective, it's extremely difficult to truly see your child as others do. Some parents avoid putting their child in any competitive situation for years in order to prevent the possibility of rejection or failure.

Here are some questions to ask yourself:

- Do you tend to assume your student is at the top of her class?
- Do you feel she deserves to be rewarded for her hard work in high school?
- Do you avoid competitive situations for your student in order to prevent possible disappointment or failure?
- Conversely, do you push your student into competitive situations to reinforce your own perceptions of her particular talents?

Many parents have already learned that it's okay to let others evaluate their son or daughter objectively. Examine how you have handled disappointing performances by your child. Did you rationalize why the results occurred or did you realign your expectations?

WHAT DO I NEED TO KNOW ABOUT MY TEENAGER?

As a parent, you are almost certainly aware by now that teenagers are emotionally volatile. One moment they're on top of the world, and the next they're feeling despondent and overwhelmed. The admissions process unfortunately can add to this emotional roller coaster. Your teenager may feel sublimely confident at one time (e.g., when she receives a good PSAT score) or devastated soon thereafter (e.g., when she gets a poor grade from a teacher "who hates me"). The fact that the process goes on for weeks, months, and years, and that there are so many levels of assessment—including grades, rigor of coursework, standardized tests, accomplishments, extracurricular activities, application essays, and teacher references—means that students begin to doubt themselves.

We've all been touched at one time by the fear of not measuring up. The fear of inadequacy is usually most powerful for children when a college denies them admission. At that point, they often take the rejection as a reflection on their competence and even their self-worth. Even before admissions decisions are announced, students may wonder out loud and to themselves if they'll make the grade. "Can I get into the school of my choice? Will the admissions committee find me sufficiently desirable?"

If your student is especially anxious about being assessed, she may act this out in many ways. You need to have your parental antennae up. Obvious underachievement can be spotted easily by grades that drop well below ability.

~We've all been touched at one time by the fear of not measuring up.~

But there are also subtle indications of fear of assessment. Your student may avoid taking standardized tests or try to limit the college selection to schools that do not require standardized tests. Sometimes this may be an accurate assessment of test-taking aptitude, but not an accurate assessment of admissions competitiveness at a particular college. Encourage your student to not sell herself short just because an ACT or SAT score is not what she had hoped. These lower scores do not preclude certain universities from being realistic possibilities.

Some students try to avoid applying to schools that require admissions essays or personal statements. This may just be a reflection of your child's "laziness." It also might signal a concern about having someone—usually unknown—evaluating her worth as a possible freshman candidate. Many colleges expect application essays not only to be creative and well written but also revealing of information about who the applicant is as a person. This can certainly be an overwhelming task for a seventeen-year-old. Who wouldn't be resistant?

WHAT DO I NEED TO KNOW AS A PARENT?

As we have mentioned, you as a parent may suffer from anxiety about how colleges will assess your son or daughter. You may begin to second-guess yourself, asking questions such as, "Did I push my child enough to work as hard as possible in high school? Should I have sent her to private school? Should we have moved to a different neighborhood?" As the application due dates get closer, you'll probably find your anxiety rising.

Consider what traits and skills colleges are actually evaluating. Yes, it's true that colleges need to look at objective measures of applicants. Certainly, grades and test scores make that easier. However, there are always going to be people who have better grades and scores than your student. You should not feel guilty about your child's SAT scores. You did not fail her, nor did she fail herself. One of the key factors in success in college and in life is determination. It's more productive to focus on what motivates your student than on worrying about her ninth grade math final.

Let's take a look at which admissions criteria cause the most concern. First, colleges will be evaluating your student's grades and the rigor of her courses. Admissions officers regularly factor in honors, Advanced Placement (AP), and International Baccalaureate (IB) classes in gauging the relative academic demands of various classes. An "A" in AP English may count as a weighted grade of "5" while an "A" in regular English may be a "4." Colleges weigh how challenging and competitive the high school is as well, even though it's not always possible to equate completely one student's experience to another. The student who gets "Bs" by consistently doing 88–89 level work may not be equivalent to a student who gets "Bs" by doing 79.8 work. Most college admissions officers understand grading procedures and grading scales at different high schools. In fact, almost all high schools submit an explanation of their grading system when they send along official student transcripts.

Next, colleges look at SAT and ACT scores. Clearly, some students have an advantage in this area because they are better test takers. Perhaps your child gets very anxious before a test, which may have a subtle but significant impact on her overall score. Many believe that self-discipline may be an even better predictor of academic success than standardized testing. However, since there is no objective measure of self-discipline, SATs remain an achievement standard for the moment.

Colleges are also looking for demonstration of special individual accomplishment. While it may seem unreasonable to expect most fifteen- to seventeen-year-olds to have excelled in a particular field by this point in their lives, many students seeking entrance to selective colleges have in fact done so. Colleges understand that some students are simply limited by geography, as there may be no lacrosse teams nearby or student orchestras or other venues for demonstrating certain skills.

Regardless of how your child will eventually fare in the admissions process, she has already begun to deal with many of life's stresses. Unfortunately, it's becoming common for teenagers to become depressed just dealing with the day-to-day struggles of high school.

One teenager in particular had a family history of depression. Her parents got divorced, and she felt overwhelmed by sadness and frustration. This in turn affected her sleep and energy level. She wanted to do well, and she tried to be motivated. But it took all her energy just to go to school, stay awake, and get her homework done. There was no room left over for commitment to any extracurricular activity. Over time, her mother helped her understand that her interest in art was a passion. The daughter very much enjoyed drawing and painting, and the mom rightly encouraged her to enroll in some elective art courses. This turned out to be good advice because her daughter's artistic interests gave her something to talk about at her college interviews.

Many teenagers are physically exhausted. Their natural biorhythm dictates that they go to sleep late and wake up late. Most teenagers don't get enough sleep because they have to get up so early to be at school. You may be fighting a losing battle by trying to get your teenager to bed earlier. Their built-in clocks usually resist bedtime before at least 11 p.m. Therefore, it's understandable why some teenagers don't become involved in extracurricular activities or community work. It's the remarkable student who can get enough sleep, succeed at school, and have enough drive and energy to excel elsewhere. Yet, in this highly competitive college market, there are plenty of teenagers who choose to try and do it all. The point for you to recognize as a parent is the need to truly know your own child and her limits. Can she function to her maximum potential on five hours of sleep? Can she do schoolwork and extracurricular activities on this schedule? Is she overloading herself and putting herself at risk for physical or emotional stress? Be realistic in assessing your own teenager's capabilities and stamina.

LEARNING TO APPRECIATE YOUR CHILD'S STRENGTHS

During the assessment phase, when you and your student are trying to decide which colleges are realistic possibilities based on her grades, scores, and accomplishments to date, you both may have to address possible unmet expectations. For example, a very bright student who never worked in high school and received mediocre grades may realize that she has blown her chances to be accepted at a highly selective university.

Penelope came from a family of two overachieving attorney parents. They provided her with every possible opportunity, from enriched summer programs to elite private schools. She had some difficulty in middle school with reading and mathematics, but her parents were able to get her tutors. When high school began, she continued to have difficulty in these subjects, though with the help of a tutor, she could have achieved an "A" average. However, given her social life and extracurricular interests, as well as a diminished interest in her studies, her academic performance fell into the "B" range. While Penelope was free to make these choices about her life and interests, her parents did not understand that these choices would have a direct impact on her future college choices. Penelope realized too late that she had limited the range of colleges at which she could realistically expect to be competitive. Her parents had not been proactive enough in monitoring her choices.

This is not an unusual scenario. In thousands of dining rooms every night, parents and students engage in lively discussions about choices. Parents need to instill the notion in their children that their current performance and activities do have implications for their future education and careers. It's not too early to begin these discussions by the time your child enters high school, especially if you and your spouse have expectations for your child to go to a top college.

You all still may feel sad, hurt, disappointed, or angry when you recognize that her options are limited. Discuss these feelings candidly while underscoring the constancy of your caring.

One true sign of maturity is recognizing and accepting being disappointed by someone you love. The college admissions experience can put that maturity to the test. It's important for you and your student to appreciate that college is just one of the many opportunities that will come her way during her lifetime.

Think about some of the movers and shakers in your hometown. Did all of them go to Duke, Cornell, or Georgetown? Were they all straight "A" students in high school? Clearly not. However, successful people at some point succeed in something. Different people can succeed at different times in their lives. While it's often viewed as a positive career move to attend a highly selective college, it doesn't necessarily guarantee success in life. Similarly, attending a non-selective college doesn't preclude success.

Another scenario that may occur during this objective assessment period is that of the average student whose parents perceive their daughter to be more talented and intellectually capable than she actually is. Most parents find it harder to acknowledge that their child may be of average ability than to believe their child is not working up to her potential. Motivation can be difficult to ascertain, and therefore it may be easier to label your student an underachiever than to accept her limits.

Try to objectively assess your daughter's work habits. How much time does she put into studying? How much effort has she put into her homework over the years?

Teachers can be an invaluable resource in helping to determine your child's true aptitude. If there is still uncertainty about your child's ability levels, you can use an educational assessment to determine if there are any learning issues impeding her development.

If done right, the search for a good match between your child and a specific college can be a wonderful learning experience. You can use the assessment aspect of the application process to bring into focus all the interests and talents of your teenager. It can be a rewarding period during which you appreciate your child's strengths. She can take pleasure in knowing what she has already accomplished in her life.

Balancing Act

Throughout your child's school years, it's important to balance encouraging her to be as successful as she can, while at the same time affirming her worth regardless of external successes or failures. This is a vital life lesson for everyone. It feels good to succeed and have others recognize those successes, but it's also crucial to develop a positive self-image regardless of external judgments.

Use the quarterly report card as a jumping-off point for a discussion regarding achievement and self-worth. While you may want to encourage your child to work harder and improve her grades, be sure to give positive feedback, too. You should convey unconditional love, regardless of her successes or failures. Sometimes this may be harder than others, but it will be worth the effort to remain supportive of your child even in the face of your own disappointment in her performance.

We can look at this through a lens of physical safety. How many parents would feel comfortable sending a young child down an expert ski slope if the child had only been skiing three times? No rational parent would put her child at such physical risk. Yet, it's quite common to repeatedly explain to children how they are destined to attend an Ivy League school even if they do not have the requisite abilities to succeed.

Many productive discussions can take place about how your child's interests and abilities might match up with future college majors and careers. Is her musical talent something she wants to continue to develop? As a professional musician? A music teacher? Or are there other interests that might supersede that one? Can your student's interest in community activism translate into some future profession? Law? Politics?

Politics is one of the areas in which parents can encourage their child to parlay her interests into a future vocational pursuit. Many students volunteer for political campaigns when they're in high school. The students who are the most engaged tend to stay involved in the political arena when they get to university. And many of these students find themselves taking campaign-related jobs after graduation, which allow them to use skills that they learned both in high school and then in college.

~If done right, the search for a good match between your child and a specific college can be a wonderful learning experience. You can use the assessment aspect of the application process to bring into focus all the interests and talents of your teenager.~

Students who are interested in art often later find themselves parlaying their artistic abilities into jobs in graphic design. There also may be less obvious paths that you can encourage your child to take. For example, if your son is an avid rock climber, you may encourage him to explore an academic field such as geology. If he can see a connection between his real-world passion and a future career, he will be more likely to work harder in school to reach his goal. This concept can be applied to many students who have nontraditional interests.

Perhaps you have a bright child who is consumed with video games to the detriment of his homework. You can try to encourage him to develop a skill in computer animation so he can develop his own future games. In the past, you may have discouraged your child's fantasizing for fear it was interfering with his performance and focus. Now you can—and should—allow him to revel in the possibilities that lie ahead.

COMING TO TERMS WITH OBJECTIVE ASSESSMENTS OF YOUR CHILD

Evaluating your child's realistic chances of gaining admission to certain schools can put your rational and irrational selves at odds. You may find yourself having discussions not only with your teenager, spouse, friends, and relatives, but also with yourself. The internal debate might go like this:

> My son is extremely bright, talented, and hard-working, and he deserves the best. On the other hand, he has a "B+" GPA and 600 on each section of the SATs, so it's probably unrealistic for him to get into an Ivy League school. On the other hand, he's as good a candidate as our neighbor's daughter, and she goes to the University of Pennsylvania. On the other hand, our neighbor's daughter was a nationally ranked tennis player, and my son is not. On the other hand, any college would be crazy not to want my son.

College admissions committees try to select students who will create an incoming freshman class that will meet the university's needs. Timing can be everything. If your child is a goalie for a hockey team, even a state champion, he still may not be recruited by top schools because they already have a freshman goalie. Instead, the college will spend its efforts recruiting a player for a different position.

This scenario is replicated at almost every college each year. There are a finite number of people who can play on the soccer or football team, or in the orchestra. Part of your child's research into exploring college options should be to examine the present and future needs of the orchestra or football team at various colleges. This information will help guide your child's choices.

University administrators frequently believe that diversity is central to the academic mission of their schools. This is a controversial issue around the country, but remains a defining element in the admissions process. Thus, from small liberal arts colleges to large universities, admissions officers attempt to draw as diverse an entering freshman class as possible.

There are an infinite number of reasons why your child may not be accepted by the college of her choice, even if on paper she appears to be a strong candidate. The number one reason, which is a painful one to internalize but true nonetheless, is the fact that the college simply wants somebody else more than they want your son or daughter. Think of it somewhat like dating. Thirty years ago, you may have had your heart set on dating the captain of the football team, but he had other plans. You probably still went to your prom, but with a different date who may have had a lower social status in your high school. How much you enjoyed the prom may have had little to do with whom you went.

It's hard for many families to understand that there is no specific list of things to do or avoid that will keep a child off the rejection list. In general, highly qualified candidates are rejected because there just is not enough space for all qualified students. Our advice is for you to encourage your child to do as well as she can in high school, but with the understanding that there are no guarantees of admission to selective colleges at the end of the road.

~College admissions committees try to select students who will create an incoming freshman class that will meet the university's needs.~

The reality is that with advanced planning most students end up at schools that are a good fit for them. Additionally, students can pursue careers and professions from a multitude of colleges and universities. Just because a student does not get into the film school at the University of Southern California does not mean she can't still become a successful filmmaker. In fact, Steven Spielberg was turned down by USC when he applied.

Exercises

One useful family exercise is to talk about each other's strengths and weaknesses. Take turns listing one another's strong points in various categories: these can be practical (e.g., she can fix things easily); emotional (he is a good listener); intellectual (she has a remarkable understanding of genetics); interpersonal (he gets along with everyone); athletic (she's a great swimmer); or artistic (he designs creative websites). You can each list your own strengths, or have family members make lists for each other. Then discuss one another's so-called weaknesses (e.g., mom is a bad cook, dad is not mechanical, son is obsessed with basketball, etc.). The intent of this exercise is not to be cruel or cause embarrassment. Rather, the goal is to focus on the reality that everyone has strengths as well as limitations.

If you're having trouble doing this, find a person in your extended family, such as an aunt, uncle, or grandparent who has a very upbeat personality and a positive attitude. Invite your relative to join you. Often a member of a different generation, such as a grandparent, can stimulate this discussion because finding positive qualities in a grandchild may come easily. Once you get going, you may find it easier to focus on each family member's positive attributes.

A good conversation starter can be for you and your spouse to share with your teenager your college admissions experiences, if you went to college. You can discuss what your applications might look like if you had to apply now. What are your strengths and liabilities? How would you choose where to apply? How would you handle having others assess your qualifications? How would you handle the possibility of rejection?

Another family exercise involves discussing someone who critiques you while also loving you (parents, best friends) and evaluations by strangers (admissions officers). The notion that we all become defensive when others criticize someone we care about is universal. For example, it's okay to criticize your own parents, but if someone else tries to (such as your spouse or a friend), you become protective. You probably feel free to critique your child's sloppiness or lack of effort in school, but you may feel hurt or defensive if an outsider makes the same observations. Understanding that outsiders may look at your child differently than you do may help prepare you for the realities of the college admissions process.

✵

If you're not prepared, the first emotional jolt to your system will probably occur when you receive the first indication of a relatively poor performance on an important component of the application process, such as a lower-than-expected SAT or ACT score. If you can anticipate that your child may not always be able to perform at the top of her game or better than her peers, you will be less anxious and frustrated.

Intellectually, you may have accepted that it's all right to objectively analyze your child's college application strengths. But if your child receives a rejection from an admissions committee, you may still feel hurt. You may know that the odds of being admitted to the most selective schools are very low. But it's quite another thing to hold a rejection letter in your hand. Parents often become enraged when their children do not get into their alma maters. Recently, a parent with a strong family legacy at a highly competitive university had a daughter who was rejected by that university. The mother was clearly more upset and offended by the rejection than the daughter.

This can be the basis of a supportive mother/daughter conversation; mom can explain that she is not disappointed in her child, but rather is upset with the college for not recognizing her daughter's strengths. Parents often respond to their child's emotional wounds, real or imagined, by becoming angry. Mom, in this case, not only felt aggrieved by her alma mater, which disappointed her, but even more important, was angry at the perceived slight toward her child.

There are many scenarios that flow from having others assess our children. Parents and children may be in denial about the realistic chances of admission to certain colleges. Or parents and children may be so reluctant to deal with possible rejection that they set their sights too low.

Here's an example of what can go wrong when a family refuses to honestly assess their teenager's qualifications for college admission. A student from a top high school in New Jersey was a "B" student, but her father had aspirations for "A-level" colleges. The girl's dad insisted that she apply to Harvard, his alma mater, as well as some other extremely competitive schools. He refused to consider suggestions of less competitive institutions. In this case, the father had always believed that it was his daughter's destiny to go to Harvard. He saw her report cards, but they did not dissuade him. He had been accepted to Harvard at a time when there were significantly fewer applications. He believed that because he had gone to Harvard, all of his children should be able to attend as well. He was totally unrealistic about the need for his daughter to consider less selective colleges even though the school guidance counselor repeatedly urged him to allow her to do so.

Intellectually, you may have accepted that it's all right to objectively analyze your child's college application strengths. But if your child receives a rejection from an admissions committee, you may still feel hurt.

The daughter did not apply to appropriate schools. She was rejected from all but one school. If the father had allowed an objective assessment to guide his daughter's choices, she would have had more options. The daughter ended up attending her safety school, which made her extremely unhappy because she now saw herself as a failure. She felt that she was a failure because only one school accepted her. In reality, her father failed her by not being objective and realistic about school choice.

Here is a different story from Nebraska. The parents of a student with mostly "As" and "Bs" and in the top 20 percent of ACT-takers nationwide, but with very weak extracurricular activities, were comfortable with their son's decision to visit only one school. He reported that he would be happy to attend this one not-overly selective college, and the parents were fairly sure that he would be accepted. By not insisting that their son at least visit other institutions, they were protecting everyone in the family from potential disappointment. Their child's decision allowed them to protect their son's self-esteem while maintaining the fantasy that he could have been accepted into Northwestern if he had applied.

While the son did gain admission and attended the less selective college, we do not recommend this as a strategy. Be realistic about possibilities, but try to explore less certain options that might inspire your child to excel even more. There is always some emotional risk in doing so, but if done in a reasonable way, such a stretch can be a growth experience.

Similarly, other parents may feel that by not looking at certain colleges, they are protecting their child from seeing a school that their child (and the parents) may want but are not able to afford. These parents look at the situation much as they would a real estate transaction: we know that we cannot afford a very expensive home in a different neighborhood, so let's not bother looking—we'll just end up being frustrated.

We don't advise this approach either. Avoid limiting initial college options based on sticker price. Who knows? You might find that an expensive school is willing to offer your child a $20,000/year scholarship. Even some very selective colleges give attractive financial aid packages to those students they really want. More than half the students in the Ivy League, for instance, receive some form of financial aid. Your child cannot be considered for aid if she doesn't apply. The same reasoning applies to scholarships in your community. We urge you to provide the materials necessary for your child to apply for as many outside scholarships as possible. Again, if you don't apply, you significantly reduce your chances of receiving outside awards.

One last story captures the extreme lengths to which some parents go to protect their children. A high school senior in California was out of town during spring break, and, while she was away, her mother intercepted the college correspondence. The student was rejected by all the highly competitive colleges she had applied to, except for one school that wait-listed her. Her mother falsely reported to her daughter by phone that the daughter had been admitted to all her colleges. However, the mother went on to say, because the family felt they would be unable to afford to send her to a private college, she (the mom) had notified the colleges that her daughter would not be able to accept the offers of admission.

The student returned to school the next week and proudly shared with her classmates and teachers that she had been accepted to Stanford, Yale, and some other top schools. The school counselor had numerous students at her door within hours, incredulous that this student had been accepted and that they, despite having higher grades and better credentials, had not. Because several of the colleges involved had notified the counselor of their admissions decisions, the counselor was able to figure out what had happened. The counselor confronted the mother. The mother refused to admit the truth to her daughter and threatened to sue the counselor if the counselor told her daughter the truth.

The obvious lesson here is to be honest with yourself and your children. Lies almost always have a way of coming back to haunt you, and they are a destructive force within any family. If and when a lie is revealed, your child will feel deceived. Often the trouble caused by the lie is worse than any distress that would have happened if the issue had been addressed forthrightly from the beginning. We especially encourage you to be honest about financial need. If there are financial limitations, make sure they are discussed from the beginning.

Encourage your child to work to his or her strengths. During the admissions process, there may be an unrealistic expectation that your child must excel in everything. Don't buy into that notion. Realistically assess your student's strengths. Universities want to know what your student can bring to the table, and for your student to have an understanding of how she can use her strengths while an undergraduate at that institution of higher learning.

There are numerous schools that fall between Princeton and your child's safety school. If you and your student carefully select a number of reasonably competitive institutions, based on an objective appraisal of the strength of your child's application, he or she is likely to have some real options after decision letters are sent out in April.

5

Establishing Realistic Expectations

As you go about establishing realistic expectations, consider your child's maturity. All adolescents do not develop at the same pace. Some demonstrate responsibility, organization, planning, and good follow-through from a relatively young age. Others are more dependent on family and friends to help them find their way. These teenagers may need constant reminding to complete tasks, and their rooms and schoolwork may be totally disorganized.

Maturity, as with so many aspects of personality, rests on a continuum. Your son is not completely mature or immature. Rather, maturity is a developing set of attitudes and abilities, including decision making, independence, and self-respect.

MATURITY LEVELS

The following are some questions you can ask yourself to determine your child's maturity level. You may want to use a scale of 1 to 10. Give your child a 1-5 for less-mature behaviors and a 6-10 for mature, responsible ones. Although there is no preset guide to what each score suggests, the results can give you a reasonably good picture of where your child is on the maturity continuum. You can also suggest to your teenager that he rate himself.

~Maturity, as with so many aspects of personality, rests on a continuum.~

67

- Has he ever held a job? Did he handle the job responsibly? Could he go to work even though the job was boring or difficult?
- How does he handle money? Does he spend it all right away? Can he delay gratification? Or does he feel compelled to buy something for himself as soon as he has pocket money?
- Does he initiate activities? Does he follow through with chores without being reminded?
- How does he handle stress?

For your teenager, you may want to pose different questions that may help him understand his own level of maturity. You can ask him to rate himself. Some questions to pose may include:

- When faced with the choice of studying for a test or watching television, which do you usually choose to do first?
- If you are struggling with an academic course, do you seek out help from anyone? Teachers? Tutors? Friends? Parents?
- When you receive money as a gift or allowance, do you spend all of it? How quickly? What do you buy with your money? Do you put money away for later use?

Your child may not want to share his answers with you; that's okay. The issues raised by these questions can still spur a healthy discussion about how you perceive his maturity level and how maturity may affect setting college expectations.

For those students who may struggle with being on their own, you may want to explore nearby schools. Even if your child begins his college education while staying at home, it can be the first step to living on campus or transferring to an out-of-town college.

If your child does consider going away to school, how far away from home do you think he can handle? If during previous away-from-home experiences, such as summer camp, your child struggled with homesickness, this may be a clue that you need to investigate schools that are within a few hours' drive or a direct plane flight away.

Will he be able to handle the stresses of group living? Dormitory life requires a certain level of maturity and social skills. Getting along with a room-mate is not an easy task. If your child is shy or lacks ease in group situations, it may be important to look at schools with varied housing options.

Will he avoid schoolwork and just play video games because he has not learned to manage his time? Time management is a vital skill for college students. If you believe that your student needs to be reminded regularly of his academic responsibilities, then consider schools and programs that offer more hands-on help and guidance.

As your student approaches high school completion, it can be a delightful family undertaking to look back on your child's early years. Sifting through photographs and watching home movies will bring back warm memories for you, as well as being a source of fascination and interest to your teenager. You can use this retrospective to explore your child's development. Was he always ahead of his peers? In walking? Talking? Reading? Catching the ball? Or was he slower to develop, maturing at a less rapid pace than his friends and relatives? How old was your teen when he reached puberty? You will probably recognize patterns that are often quite consistent. Thus, you will have a jump start on recognizing your child's current maturity level as well as a clearer understanding of how he moves from one developmental stage to another.

DISABILITY ISSUES

Be realistic about what, if any, support systems may need to be in place for your student. If your child has been receiving services for a learning disability, be sure to factor this into his college choices. If possible, fully address the nature and degree of any learning problems.

Students with learning issues will usually need a recent (within the last three years) battery of psychological tests in order to be eligible for services at college. If your student hopes to obtain extra time on the SATs, provide educational evaluations to the College Board with plenty of lead time. Many times the College Board will turn down such requests—and you'll want enough time to appeal the decision before the actual test date.

Specifically, we urge you to complete this educational assessment no later than the beginning of sophomore year. This gives you the ability to use the assessment results for standardized tests taken during your child's sophomore or junior year of high school.

Recognizing learning limitations that your student may have is critical for establishing realistic college goals. Special education services can be helpful for many students. Being realistic about the type of school and the services those colleges or universities offer will likely make the difference between a successful and unsuccessful transition to college.

Medical Needs

An often-overlooked issue in determining appropriate college options is the assessment of a student's possible medical needs. These may range from apparently benign seasonal allergies to more significant concerns such as diabetes or bipolar disorder.

The nature and quality of healthcare on campus should be taken into consideration. Can your child easily and comfortably access student health services? If your child requires weekly allergy shots, can the school provide them? What is the availability of healthcare off campus? Is there a hospital nearby? Can your student easily get to a doctor's office, especially if freshmen are not allowed to have vehicles on campus? Is there public transportation? And will all this be too time consuming and complicated for your student to navigate the system?

An often-overlooked issue in determining appropriate college options is the assessment of a student's possible medical needs.

Serious chronic illnesses need to be closely monitored. Does your student have the maturity and responsibility to manage his own healthcare? Parents often worry about their teenager going off to college and engaging in risky behavior. However, this risky behavior may be as simple as neglecting chronic health issues.

Heather and Diabetes

Heather had juvenile diabetes. She was extremely bright, performed exceedingly well in high school, and had planned to attend a highly competitive university. After being accepted to a top-tier school, she and her family did some soul searching and came to the conclusion that she was not comfortable being an airplane ride away from home and her doctors. She decided to attend a college that was within a manageable driving distance from home. Her anxiety lifted once she made this decision.

Max and Cerebral Palsy

Max had mild cerebral palsy that impaired his motor functioning, affecting his speech and mobility. Over the years, he developed confidence in his ability to navigate independently, even though it took him longer to get places and be understood. He also used technology to minimize the impact of his disability on his academic performance.

He was an excellent student and chose to apply to leading colleges throughout the country. His parents were very concerned about his being on his own, and they discouraged his applications to schools far away. However, when he was accepted by several selective schools, he was able to convince his parents that he could do well on his own. On his own, he researched the school living arrangements, counseling, and other support services that he would need. By demonstrating to his parents his maturity, he earned their confidence, and they were willing to let him leave home.

Psychological Services

Another concern may be the need for psychological services. If your student has been in therapy, you may want to begin discussions with her therapist about how to transfer care to another mental-health professional. You may have to investigate services available on or near various campuses. What does the school offer? Is there a counseling center and what is the quality?

In high-quality campus psychological services, the counselors are proactive and have a system whereby they regularly contact students. This is preferable to the laissez-faire counseling center models. Ask how, when, and where the counseling staff connects with students.

Additionally, try to meet directly with a member of the counseling service. Don't rely on information presented at general college information sessions. Find out how regular appointments can be scheduled. How private would it feel for your child to be seen by a therapist in student health? Are there limits to the services that on-campus therapists are willing to provide? Are there well-qualified professionals off-campus?

Marianne and Depression

Marianne suffered from clinical depression. Despite making excellent progress and greatly reducing symptoms through therapy and medication, she was concerned about being on her own, far from her support systems. She explored options with her family, and together they decided to work toward a realistic plan. Eventually, she recognized that she wanted a small school, where she felt she could get her needs met rapidly should she experience problems. After this appropriate exploration, she selected and later was accepted to a small school with strong student support services.

In general, schools with smaller student-to-faculty ratios are better positioned to provide more intense and regular counseling services. There is an argument to be made, however, that big universities with large budgets are able to hire more support staff. In either case, examine how students can, and do, have contact with counselors on a particular campus.

WHAT DO I NEED TO KNOW AS A PARENT?

While you as a parent may be eager to act in the capacity of advisor and supporter of your child, it's important to keep reminding yourself that it's your son or daughter who will be going to college. While this may be stating the obvious, many of us find it difficult to disengage ourselves emotionally from this process. While helping our teens with the ins and outs of the admissions process, we need to differentiate between what would be appealing to us and what is appealing to them.

Some of you may have had few options regarding where you could go to college, given the economic demands on your family. Thus, you may feel proud that you have the opportunity to offer experiences to your children that you did not have.

Others of you may have experienced college as the best years of your life. At college, you may have met not only the people who have remained your best friends, but you may also have met your spouse. You may be thrilled that your son or daughter could have the opportunity to experience the same freedoms, excitement, and opportunities that you had—maybe even at the same university.

Whatever your perspective, this is the point at which you must rein in your own emotions and recognize that this is not going to be your college experience. Rather, you are helping your child to select a place where she can make her own experiences and memories. While we all derive certain vicarious pleasures from our children's experiences, especially those that we never had, we must keep reminding ourselves that it's their lives to lead, not ours.

Separating Your Experience from Your Child's

Here are some questions to ask yourself to help assess if you are living through your child:

▶ Do you find yourself daydreaming about your own college experiences? Do you wish you had gone somewhere else—maybe where your daughter is considering applying?
▶ Do you remember your SAT scores off the top of your head?
▶ Do you remember where you applied and where you were admitted?
▶ Do you find yourself planning how frequently you may want to visit your child at college?
▶ Are you asking your child intrusive questions about the details of her social life?

You may have already experienced the vicarious joy of your daughter playing a varsity sport or getting the lead in the high school play. Later, you may have had to accept your child's decision to quit the team or stop acting, for lack of interest or time. You may have almost felt betrayed by your

~While we all derive certain vicarious pleasures from our children's experiences, especially those that we never had, we must keep reminding ourselves that it's their lives to lead, not ours.~

child's abandonment of what, to you, seemed like an exciting and worthwhile enterprise. But if your teenager truly no longer feels that way herself, you have to respect that decision.

In terms of the college admissions process, you have to learn to recognize what your issues are and what your teenager's are. For example, if you always felt you missed out on belonging to a sorority, you need to be sensitive to the fact that your daughter may not share your views. Alternatively, you may need to learn to feel comfortable with your student's focus on Greek life as an important component of her college selection.

College generations change every four years. A college can have a significantly different social vibe in just a few years, let alone in thirty. We all know that the country can shift politically to the left or right and can go through good economic times and bad. Colleges, as an integral part of our society, reflect these shifts in attitudes and behavior. But the reality is that today's college students have to navigate the social life on campus as they experience it in the present, not as their parents experienced it in the past.

Adolescence is a period of growth during which it's absolutely appropriate for teenagers to assert how they are different from their parents. One way to do this may be in their college choices. You may feel that the only worthwhile degree in higher education has a pre-professional emphasis, but your student may insist on looking at liberal arts colleges that focus on more theoretical aspects of academic disciplines.

If you push your position and values too strongly, your child may believe he has no emotional recourse but to disagree with all your points—no matter how valid they may be. If you know that your child has a tendency to introversion and is more comfortable in smaller settings, you may suggest that he should consider only small schools. However, if you insist on the "truth" of your position, your child may insist he wants to attend only a large university.

Exercise

Here's a family exercise that not only explores realistic expectations regarding college selection, but also helps to defuse parent-child tension regarding whose criteria and expectations should be followed. You and your student should each make a list of twenty important variables to be considered when selecting a college. Next to each variable, indicate whether or not you believe this is a valuable aspect of college (e.g., size of school, selectivity of school, being able to play a varsity sport at college, etc.).

Then compare notes with your child. Where do you share the same expectations? Where are they different? Can you accept what is important to your teenager, even if some items on the top of his list didn't make your list? Can you accept what is important to your student even if you totally disagree with some of his wish list items?

Individualize Each Child's College Search Experience

Make sure you're able to individualize your expectations for each of your children. If you have already launched one or more of your children to college, remind yourself that each is probably quite different from the others. Even though you might like to put the college admissions process on auto-pilot, you'll still need to go through the appropriate exploration of realistic needs and expectations for the child now going through the process.

Just because you learned all about the Big Ten universities for your older son does not mean that they will be a good fit for your daughter. Not only do you need to evaluate the individual market positions of your children based upon the strength of their applications, you also need to address their unique interests, personalities, and educational and career goals. Some families can use the same information for each of their children, especially if certain constraints remain constant. An example of this would be continuing to limit college options to in-state public universities. But it's usually a good idea to anticipate that you will be examining different strengths and learning objectives for each of your children.

Even if you have gone through the college admissions process before with another child, information is constantly changing. For example, a relatively new admissions option is early decision II, a plan under which a college evaluates applications from students who are generally committed to attending that college if admitted. Early decision II is essentially the same as early decision—except it's eight or ten weeks later. For some students, this is an attractive option. Those who are keen to finish the admissions process early now have two early decision opportunities. Another thing to look out for: changes in the SAT and ACT. These tests have added essay sections, and the procedures for requesting extra time change relatively frequently. Therefore, make sure you continue to do your homework for your second child.

This is the first time your present high school student is exploring his options for college. It would be unfair to shortchange him of the opportunity to use the college search as a vehicle to learn more about himself and what he wants from a college education. Sometimes, second or third children use the previous college searches of their older siblings as a way to avoid putting any energy or effort into the process. Do not allow him to be lazy about the process. Encourage campus visits and exploration of what's currently available. With thousands of colleges and universities to choose from, each of your children can explore in different directions. Ultimately, some of your children may attend the same schools, which is certainly all right. However, it's important that they select the same schools for good reasons, not just because it is easier.

WHAT DO I NEED TO KNOW ABOUT MY TEENAGER?

One hallmark of adolescence is difficulty in remaining on task. The nature of a teenager is to be easily distracted. Even daily chores and homework assignments may become lost in the process of just getting through the day. Exciting news regarding relationships, such as new girlfriends or the anticipation of after-school events, may take your child off task.

Many adolescents are incapable of planning. While they may perceive themselves as invincible, at the same time, they lack the ability to anticipate future events or feelings. Getting a ninth grader to start considering what courses he may want to take next semester might be as far into the future as your child is able or willing to look. Asking your child to start thinking about college decisions or possible career options may elicit looks that could turn you to stone. Your teenager may react with anger, possibly arguing, "Why are you pestering me about something that won't take place for

Even if you have gone through the college admissions process before with another child, information is constantly changing.

years?" Or he might regard you as if you have three heads, reacting with profound stupefaction stating, "Anyone in their right mind knows you don't have to plan that far in advance." Or he may react with anxiety and tension, feeling you are putting undue pressure upon him. He may feel that he is unprepared to even start thinking about college. Any discussions regarding the future may trigger an emotionally charged response.

It is possible that your adolescent will be totally evasive about the subject of college admissions. Parents often assume that because they're enthusiastic about the prospect of their children going off to college, their students feel the same way. We also tend to feel that because we understand that this event calls for long-range planning, our teenagers will too. How wrong we might be!

Frequently, the first college-related struggle with your child involves just trying to get his attention. You already know how difficult it can be to get him to focus on daily tasks. How long does it take to get your teenager off the computer to go to bed? Or off the telephone to eat dinner? Often, our requests fall on deaf ears. Now think about trying to get him to attend to a process that may start many months ahead of what he perceives is the correct timeline. It can be a struggle of epic proportions.

Getting Your Teen to Cooperate

Assess how willing a partner your teenager is with you regarding the college admissions process. Determine where your teenager may fall on the continuum of willingness to plan ahead. Is she organized? Does she procrastinate? Does she do her chores on time? Has she already, independent of you, begun to express an interest in the college admissions process? Does she discuss the future? Does she already have career plans, tentative though they may be?

Once you have an adequate appraisal of your child's willingness to explore her future, you can begin to engage in the process together. But what happens if your teenager is totally disinterested in college admissions planning, at least at this time? Here are several suggestions:

First, try to find some aspect of college that can engage your child. For example, if she is a sports enthusiast, talk about colleges in terms of collegiate athletics. Attend college varsity games in your area. Or, if your child has a particular talent, such as music, attend a student music recital at a nearby college. If she enjoys traveling, suggest the possibility of visiting different college campuses while on family trips. Whenever you can think of something to engage your reluctant teen, give it a try.

Second, take whatever complaints your child has about high school and turn them into positives about college. If your student feels that the classes in high school are boring, start discussing what it could be like at college, when she gets to choose almost all her own courses.

Third, take general complaints about life (i.e., too many high school classes, overly strict parents, etc.) and discuss how things will be different at college. The experience of living independently in a dormitory is a unique opportunity. Play this up for your teenager, and you're likely to pique her interest at some level.

Managing Time and Tasks

Let's face it. The college admissions process in its current design takes a tremendous amount of physical and emotional time and energy. Many families will spend hundreds of hours discussing colleges, visiting colleges, and making sure applications get out the door. Most families do not have hundreds of hours to spare, so it's imperative to focus on the most important tasks. Reserve time now for future college visits. Visiting campuses becomes very expensive and very frustrating when done at the last minute. There's almost never a convenient time to pick up and spend three days touring colleges, but such visits will help your child understand the subtle and not-so-subtle differences between various colleges. Often parents find that it's easier to plan college visits around business trips or family vacations. If such scheduling makes it easier for your family to get on the road, then we support it.

In terms of the applications themselves, we advise you to do less worrying and more hands-on review of the process. While we don't mean to minimize the emotional component of what your child's college prospects mean for you, helping her complete the applications in a timely fashion is far more important than worrying about what might happen if the applications are not completed on time.

Many parents find they do not have as much time as they need to thoroughly supervise this process. Your high school guidance counselor or independent educational consultant can be of assistance. Even if you do rely heavily on others, you as the parent still have the ultimate responsibility to make sure this process runs smoothly.

For the students who are excited about college as early as the ninth grade, we applaud this. Encourage your child to visit and think about her long-term academic interests as soon as she's comfortable. There's almost no danger in beginning the admissions process early if done carefully and responsibly. Serious students who want to begin the process early are often very focused. Follow their lead. If your child asks to visit a college or wants to discuss university majors with you, feel free to do so. Enjoy being able to take your cues from your child. If you have a motivated student, appreciate her enthusiasm and focus.

ASSESSING THE EVER-CHANGING NEEDS OF INDIVIDUAL COLLEGES AND UNIVERSITIES

In the increasingly complex and confusing world of college admissions, perhaps the most disturbing component is the difficulty students and parents have in distinguishing between realistic and nonrealistic expectations. What colleges want and expect from their incoming freshman class often feels like a moving target. What seemed desirable a couple of years ago may no longer be particularly desirable this year. For instance, one leading university for a few years was looking to dramatically increase the number of students from Colorado. Once a sizable group of Coloradans was in place, the school moved on to other recruiting areas. Moreover, a college can easily end up with too many economics majors—which might cause the school to try to accept fewer prospective economics students the following year.

There's such a thing, though, as being too clever as it relates to the admissions process. It would be extremely dangerous not to apply to a specific economics program because you fear there might be too many other applicants. As with most things in life, there are pros and cons about applying to the most popular major on campus. Your student must assess how strong

~What colleges want and expect from their incoming freshman class often feels like a moving target. What seemed desirable a couple of years ago may no longer be particularly desirable this year.~

his interest is in such a field and whether he's competitive with other applicants. Be careful. Some students in this situation simply put down on their application that they're interested in studying ancient Greek literature because they know that less popular departments are seeking new undergraduate students. This rarely works unless your student has been studying ancient Greek for the past few years.

The moving goal post frustrates even the best of parent-planners. As you and your student try to objectively assess the strength of his application, it becomes more difficult to realistically determine what to expect. Ask your high school guidance counselor to help. Be aware, though, that not all high school counseling offices are geared to long-range college planning.

Look at the number of students that each counselor is responsible for and the physical resources of the college counseling office itself. Does your high school guidance counselor meet with you regularly to review your child's progress? Is your high school guidance counselor available to meet with you and your spouse about college selection and any concerns you may have along the way? Does your counselor regularly visit universities to keep abreast of changes taking place on various campuses?

The most unrealistic expectations generally have to do with the prestige of various colleges. Many families fail to understand that it's fiercely competitive to be admitted to some of the name-brand universities in the United States. There are over 25,000 high schools in the United States. Each one has a math superstar, a soccer stand-out, and a computer whiz. Your child will now be competing on a national and international scale. It's crucial that you help your child assess his realistic chances of being admitted to various schools.

Understanding Timelines and the Competition

There are important timelines involved in the admissions process. While some families make the mistake of thinking they don't have to arrive at any decisions prior to the fall of senior year, you should begin the task of planning for the process months—and years—earlier. It can often take several years to lay the groundwork for successful applications.

Plan to finish standardized testing by the spring of junior year so that your child can devote the time in the fall of senior year to completing his college applications without having to study for the SATs. Pay particular attention to the SAT Subject Tests, which some colleges require in order to assess student achievement in specific areas of study. If your teenager takes biology sophomore year, for instance, he might take the SAT Subject Test in biology at that point. Often school guidance counselors fail to inform students and parents of the option of taking SAT Subject Tests before junior year. Even if there is only a slim chance that your child may want to apply to colleges where these tests are required for admission, it's better to take them when the academic material is still fresh.

Your student may want to assess his testing strengths and weaknesses before he decides whether to take the SAT or the ACT. Some students who have never been good test takers find that the ACT gives them the chance to shine in individual academic subjects—in a way that the aptitude-based SAT does not. There are countless pros and cons about this subject; we advise you to seek the counsel of testing experts who can assess your child individually.

Understanding how timelines affect your child's applications is absolutely necessary. Applying early decision or rolling admissions may be critical to an optimum outcome. Thus, having all your ducks in a row, including testing, letters of recommendation, essays, college visits, and financial discussions, may need to happen much sooner than you originally thought.

~There are over 25,000 high schools in the United States. Each one has a math superstar, a soccer stand-out, and a computer whiz.~

The rule of thumb is that all college applications should be sent in before your high school senior begins winter break. By submitting applications earlier, students are in a position to qualify for more funding and possibly have their admissions applications reviewed sooner. Many universities process applications as soon as they are received. This is true even if schools don't advertise an early review of applications. Universities have the power to accept a student as soon as they become convinced that he will be able to contribute significantly to the incoming freshman class.

Why not have an answer sooner rather than later? Think of this a little like buying an airplane ticket. The longer you wait, the fewer good seats will be available. Starting the process early can help you establish realistic expectations much sooner than those families who simply throw applications out into cyberspace and wait until April to see how they land.

Financial Concerns and Expectations

Money has to be considered whenever the topic of realistic expectations regarding college admissions is discussed. Although many people tend to avoid addressing possible financial constraints, we encourage you to begin to develop a plan as early as possible.

The application process itself can be costly. Signing up for the SATs, tutoring, educational consulting, and trips to colleges can run into thousands of dollars. Applications at $50 to $100 per college also add to expenses.

> ~The rule of thumb is that all college applications should be sent in before your high school senior begins winter break.~

Tuition at some private universities already tops $35,000 per year, which does not even cover room, board, books, travel, and other living expenses. Therefore, it's not unreasonable to anticipate investing $150,000-$200,000 in your child's education, before any scholarships or student loans. For most people, this is an enormous amount of money. You and your family need to determine if you're able and willing to make this investment.

Less expensive options exist, but it's not always easy to be accepted to the great universities with great prices. Some schools are entirely subsidized, like the military academies, but it can be exceedingly difficult to gain a seat at many of these institutions. In general, state universities for out-of-state students cost approximately half of what a comparable private university costs. Attending an in-state state institution will cut costs in half again. Keep in mind, though, that the costs of boarding and food are usually not insignificant—even at state schools in your home state.

Regardless of which types of schools your student may consider, cost may set the foundation for other considerations. Therefore, in addition to objectively assessing your child's market position for gaining admission, you also need to realistically assess your financial situation.

Financial Questions to Answer:

- What can our family afford to spend on college over four years?
- Do we have other children and will we be able to spend the same amount on each of our children, if they all go to college?
- What have we saved for their education already?

▶ How much are we willing to save/spend from our annual income each year in order to pay for higher education?

▶ Are we prepared for a continued 5 to 10 percent increase in college costs over the next several years?

▶ Will we rely on financial aid to make ends meet?

▶ Have we familiarized ourselves with the formulas for obtaining financial aid?

▶ Have we considered that most financial aid is in the form of student loans—as opposed to grants?

▶ How do we and our student feel about his coming out of college with substantial financial debt?

BE PROACTIVE

With little outside guidance or joint family exploration, some students randomly select colleges and universities to which they decide to apply. The selections appear to make little sense. Geographically, they may be all over the country and of different sizes, and offer totally different educational and social experiences. Sometimes it seems as if the students just heard about these schools; maybe they liked the names, or maybe someone they knew went there and liked a particular school. The attitude is similar to throwing darts at a list of schools and randomly applying to those on which the darts land. Then, decisions are deferred until April of senior year when students receive letters of acceptance and rejection.

Rather than taking the random approach, we urge you and your student to be thoughtful, proactive consumers. Establish realistic expectations—for what your teenager wants from his college experience, what you can afford, and which schools would be a good fit. Some high schools force you to do this by allowing students to apply to only a limited number of universities. Most high schools, however, do not have these application restrictions—leaving it to your child to determine which, and how many, institutions to apply to. Regardless of your high school's policy, you and your teenager still have to do a lot of exploring and decision making in the quest for colleges that will be right for your child.

Try to get a realistic assessment of your child's college options. You don't want your student to set his sights too high or too low. Ideally, your teenager should apply to a combination of schools, some that are more selective and others that are less selective. Focus on schools to which your student wants to apply, where he believes he can be happy, and where many of his requirements for a college can be met.

6

Fear of Failure

We all know what it feels like to fail. Maybe we recall failing our first spelling test in elementary school, or our disappointment when we failed to make the varsity track team or get a part in the high school play. Sometimes we feel failure in the pit of our stomachs; sometimes we're filled with embarrassment or guilt at letting someone else down. However we experience the emotion, it's a feeling we try to avoid. Many of us take great pains to steer clear of situations that may lead to failure.

The college admissions process is replete with possibilities to experience a sense of failure. While nobody actually fails in the true sense of the word—almost every student who wants to attend college will be able to find a school where she will be accepted—the college admissions process still elicits tremendous anxiety, often as a result of parents and children fearing failure.

There are pressures mounting from all sides: friends, neighbors, your children's friends' parents, teachers, coaches, grandparents, and almost everyone else you meet, whether standing in line at the grocery store or while attending a dinner party. When people know you're the parent of a high school sophomore, junior, or senior, virtually the first question out of their mouths is, "Where is your daughter thinking about going to college?"

This period in a family's life, in which outside pressures are so strongly brought to bear, is rivaled only by pregnancy. As you're sure to recall, people feel they have unlimited license to ask any and all personal questions about your body (or your wife's body). You probably also can recall a situation in which someone, often a stranger, made you feel anxious. Have you read the latest data on certain medications? Is it safe to fly? To drive? To exercise? There were subtle, and not so subtle, pressures to conform. What baby equipment are you going to purchase? Who is your doctor? Are you going through natural childbirth? What are you going to do for childcare? What would be considered rude and inappropriate in almost any other situation somehow appears socially acceptable to many people when they see a pregnant woman.

The same phenomenon occurs when you're the parent of a high school student. All questions about her future are up for grabs: How did she do on the SATs? Are you taking her to a tutor? What colleges are you considering? Is your child applying early decision? Even if you feel confident that you're going to be immune to these outside pressures, you'll find it nearly impossible to completely avoid the fear that you and your student will not measure up.

Personal expectations, peer and social pressures, and financial issues are just some of the sources of stress and fears of inadequacy. When faced with so many options, numerous opinions, and a multiplicity of paths to follow, it's natural to experience anxiety about the decision-making process.

WHAT DO I NEED TO KNOW AS A PARENT?

Once you become a parent, your perspective on success and failure may shift. During your own childhood, adolescence, and young adulthood, you may have developed a sound sense of yourself and your abilities. You had to live through your own personal failures. In time, perhaps you came to realize that you could survive them. You may even have come to advise others that nothing can be gained if you don't at least try.

For some of us, though, failure is never an acceptable alternative. We experience failure as a blow to our self-esteem. Whether you failed to get the job you were really hoping for, or you failed to anticipate traffic congestion and were late for a date, you still may shudder at the thought of not being successful.

Those of us who are perfectionists truly suffer from the fear of failure. We dread it, and yet are confronted with unlimited opportunities to experience it every day. Almost any task may elicit dread that we won't be able to make the grade. If we get an "A" on a paper, we may feel we failed because we didn't receive an "A+."

Some of us who dread failure choose to become what many refer to as underachievers. The notion is that if we don't try, we can't fail. If you fear that sense of failure, you may find yourself not participating in some activity or endeavor. For example, if you feel awful losing a tennis match, you may give up playing rather than risking defeat. If you fear you won't get the promotion, you may avoid applying for it. Psychologically, if you don't risk sticking your neck out, you can't get it chopped off. Sometimes we refer to this as playing safe. But it can be a powerful method for many of us to feel that we're still in control.

~Those of us who are perfectionists truly suffer from the fear of failure. We dread it, and yet are confronted with unlimited opportunities to experience it every day.~

If you choose not to spend a lot of time and effort in your garden, and then nothing grows well, you can feel okay about yourself. In such a case, you made the limited time commitment and were in control of how much of yourself you were willing to put into the task. If it doesn't work out very well, you can feel fine with that outcome. However, if you spend hours weeding, watering, feeding, and tending to your garden, and it still fails, your personal sense of investment would be on the line. You would experience failure, even though you tried your hardest.

As with other aspects of your teenager's development, it's healthy to explore your own feelings about failure and your own outlook on how to approach situations that may lead to disappointment. Before entering the college search, you need to recognize your own and your child's Achilles' heel as it relates to success and failure.

The admissions process is far more nuanced than this, but there are pressures that often make it feel like an all-or-nothing experience. Namely, you and your student may feel sucked into believing that she is successful only if she gets into every college to which she applies, or only if she gains admission to her first-choice college. How you feel about what constitutes success and how you handle life's failures will shed a bright light on how your child may process her own experiences.

A key point to remember: almost all students take their acceptances and rejections more in stride than do their parents. Your child will not break in two if she doesn't get into Harvard. Yes, encourage your teenager to do the best application possible, but understand that every year over 85 percent of the terrific students who apply to Harvard are rejected. We dare say that you would be proud to be the parent of most of these rejected Harvard applicants.

One mother a few years ago insisted that her son get a six-year Bachelor of Science/Doctor of Medicine (BS/MD) degree. BS/MD programs are highly valued programs that enable students to secure a place in medical school while they are still in high school. In the eyes of many students and parents, this program saves a student from having to go through the medical school admissions process in a few years' time. As long as a student maintains a certain grade point average in his undergraduate courses, he's automatically enrolled in that university's medical program. Of course, this dual program is designed for those who are certain that they want to be doctors.

Here's the downside: most universities do not have such a dual program, and those that do often have only fifteen or twenty spaces per year. As you might imagine, admission is extremely competitive to a BS/MD program.

The sheer competition for spaces did not deter this particular mother, who saw only success and failure in this process. Such a black-and-white view was not helpful to her son, who, unfortunately, was not really a competitive applicant for such programs. A slightly more nuanced view of the pre-med world would have shown the mother that her son could have gone to numerous universities as a pre-med student, from where he could then apply to medical school—after he had a few years of solid college grades under his belt.

Rarely is it the case that only one college will help your child grow as a person. One family in New York became so caught up in the hype about a particular college that they failed to appreciate there are other colleges with relatively similar characteristics. Yes, the Massachusetts Institute of Technology offers a unique academic experience in the desirable Boston area. But Cal Tech, Georgia Tech, and Rensselaer offer similar academic programs that in some areas surpass MIT's.

As a caring parent, you realize you're emotionally wrapped up in your child's successes and failures. For each soccer goal scored, you may experience the euphoria of success, or your child's straight-"A" report card may make you swell with pride. Of course, you know such successes are due to your child's efforts, but we all take some ownership whenever our child makes us proud.

Conversely, we also are emotionally invested when our children fail. We feel their pain when they're disappointed with failing to make good enough grades to take honors-level courses. Or we may feel the bitter sting when they fail to gain admission to a particular independent school or summer program. While we may try to explain to our children that the disappointment will fade, often we have as much, if not more, difficulty getting past the hurt than our children do.

What constitutes failure can mean different things for different families. For some, it has to do with the financial investment in higher education. Mr. Inello looked at college as an investment in his daughter's future. He felt that since his daughter "only" wanted to be an elementary school teacher, he would not spend any money exploring the options of her attending a private or out-of-state university. Even though she had strong grades, good activities, and good SAT scores, the father was adamant. He was not willing to explore the possibility of greater investment (whether in the form of loans or more parental underwriting) in her possible intellectual growth and emotional development. Her career goal was such that she was almost certain to "fail" him, because such a career would make it financially impossible for the family to make back the higher education investment.

Even without such a stark view of the world, thousands of families decide every day whether particular investments make sense for them. One middle-class family was fortunate to have a bright son who was attracted to the University of Chicago because of its intellectual reputation. After much discussion, the family decided to allow their son to apply. The good news was that he was admitted. The bad news was that the family would now have to figure out how to pay the tuition.

~What constitutes failure can mean different things for different families.~

The parents never once spoke in front of their son about the hoped-for return on investment, even though they were concerned that their son could end up in significant debt from student loans—without serious prospects for a way to repay the loans. The family talked through the pros and cons of going to a school such as the University of Chicago, and ultimately decided that the cost was worth it.

WHAT DO I NEED TO KNOW ABOUT MY TEENAGER?

Once you understand how you and your spouse handle failure or the fear of failure, you can shift your focus to your child. How does your son or daughter approach the possibility of failure?

We believe you should help your child at least try to reach for some of her dreams. Be sure to speak with your teenager about failure—and explain to her that you will continue loving and supporting her if she fails to be admitted to certain colleges.

Samantha and Underachievement

Samantha was a very bright young woman. However, despite her good test scores, she had very low grades. She performed at a minimal level during high school, and she made it clear she didn't want to work hard in college either. At every school selection meeting with her counselor and parents, she was interested only in finding out which colleges were the least demanding academically. Her immaturity shone through clearly. She was afraid to truly apply herself, most likely because she was afraid to fail. She ended up attending a college that did not challenge her academically.

Frank and Taking Chances

After visiting almost a dozen colleges, Frank decided to apply early decision to one of the more competitive institutions on his list. His parents told him that they would be supportive of him and would still love him if he failed to be admitted. When the letter arrived and informed Frank that he was deferred, his parents explained to Frank that there were likely to be other good options for him in the spring. When spring rolled around, Frank was indeed admitted to a number of colleges, but was wait-listed at his original top choice. He then went back to see some of the schools that had admitted him and came to a tentative decision. He informed his parents that he was going to choose one of the colleges that he had just revisited.

The next week, Frank visited his soon-to-be college one more time. He went to classes and parties there. He stayed overnight with a student. He signed up for freshman housing and bought the requisite T-shirt. He returned home and began planning for his college career.

Then something interesting happened. His original first-choice school called and invited him to be a member of the incoming freshman class. Frank was stunned. He was excited to receive the call, but he had already emotionally settled on attending a different college. His parents left the decision to him. After just two days, Frank told his parents that he was not going to alter his college plans. He was pleased with his decision, and the fact that he now was admitted to his original first-choice college was irrelevant.

~Fear of failure is inextricably tied up with loss of control. You and your child are not in control because someone else is going to judge your student's value.~

The tremendous emotional roller coaster had finally come to a stop. The outcome could easily have been different, but the parental support he received throughout the process gave Frank the strength to come to his decision.

THE COLLEGE ADMISSIONS PROCESS AND LOSS OF CONTROL

Fear of failure is inextricably tied up with loss of control. You and your child are not in control because someone else is going to judge your student's value. Someone else will decide whether your child will be accepted to a certain college or university. This loss of control can have a tremendous impact on both of you, depending on your level of emotional maturity and ego strength.

The more emotionally mature your student is, the greater the likelihood she'll be able to separate the notion of failure to gain admission to college from failure as a person. You can serve as a positive role model during this period. By not letting your own ego become enmeshed in the selection process, you'll be able to provide tremendous support and grounding to your teenager. It's crucial to state and restate the obvious: whether or not one is accepted to a college is not a reflection of self-worth. Your being the continual bearer of this message will be invaluable to your child. Life will go on, regardless of the outcome of the college admissions process.

7

Enhancing Your Family's Communication

We've discussed the many variations on a theme that can lead families to struggle over the college admissions process. Yet, there are many ways in which you can use this experience to bring your family together. This doesn't have to be a process that wrenches families apart. Despite the often intense emotionality of this period, it's possible to enjoy and even revel in the many aspects of this pathway to your teenager's college years.

Be aware of your communication styles. Are you sharing information in a way that others in the family can hear it? As a parent or spouse, are you unclear or indecisive? Do you or other family members "forget" to share critical information? These are just a few questions to consider as you try to understand the essential ingredients for good communication and conflict minimization.

ASSESS YOUR FAMILY'S COMMUNICATION STYLE

Let's take a look at how your family communicates right now. There is no right or wrong way, but good communication is key to the health of any and all relationships. When families fail to communicate, trouble is usually not far behind. As we've seen from our discussion so far, the ability to share information is crucial to the success of the college admissions process. Not only do you and your child need to communicate about high school courses, extracurricular interests, and long-term goals, but you also need to share information with counselors, teachers, and college admissions personnel as well.

The following is an eight-item questionnaire designed to help you and your family think about the "who, what, where, when, and how" of your communication. Answer each item not only for how you as an individual tend to communicate, but also how your family as a unit communicates. Additionally, each member of your family may want to take this questionnaire individually. Then feel free to compare notes and see how similar or dissimilar you are in your communication styles.

1. Do you tend to be more open or closed in the way you share information?

If you have an open style of communication, there's a free flow of information. You're comfortable sharing information and believe it's important to keep one another aware of what's happening. You discuss what goes on in the present, as well as making a point to discuss future plans. This open style cuts across generational lines as well as between generations—you talk not only with your spouse or significant other and friends, but also with children and parents.

If you have a closed style of communication, you have more limited patterns of communication. You may reflect on who has a need to know. You may be more willing to share information within generations than across generations. You may also be more willing to communicate with some people than with others. You may communicate information only after decisions have been made rather than use discussions as a vehicle to help you formulate decisions. Your child may communicate primarily with only one parent or only with siblings.

2. Is your communication direct or indirect?

Some of us avoid being direct in our communication, often for fear of antagonizing or upsetting the other person. For example, instead of asking for help directly, you may say to your spouse, "I am so exhausted." Your spouse is supposed to recognize that this means you want more assistance.

Unless your significant other has learned your communication cues, he or she may be too tired or unfocused to grasp your intent. This may, in turn, lead you to feel hurt, uncared for, or even angry.

People sometimes avoid direct communication because they fear not being heard or supported. Perhaps your daughter tells you that her teacher assigned a really "stupid" book. She may mean that she's having trouble understanding it but is embarrassed to ask for help.

The less directly a person communicates facts and feelings, the greater the likelihood of misinterpretation. Almost all of us remember playing the game of telephone. One person whispers something in the second person's ear. The second person, in turn, whispers what he heard into the next person's ear. This continues until everyone in the group has "received" the message. The more people the message goes through, the more likely it is to be distorted. This can be what happens in families that use indirect communication.

The clearer and briefer the message is at the beginning of "telephone," the more likely it will be transmitted accurately. Try to state what you want, feel, or need to other family members as clearly and concisely as possible. By doing so, you leave less room for miscommunication, which in turn will produce less conflict.

3. What information is shared and with whom?

You can probably recognize your patterns of sharing information if you take a minute to consider them. Often, we choose to share the same types of information with certain people. Perhaps you share neighborhood gossip and discuss the teachers in your student's school with friends. However, you may choose not to share information about your own child's academic successes and failures with the same friends. But there may be some people with whom you do share this information, possibly even total strangers you meet on an airplane. Strangers provide us with a sense of anonymity and can offer confidentiality that we often do not feel with our friends and relatives.

Each of us develops a comfort zone with regard to what we broadcast. Sometimes all family members are on the same wavelength, and everyone is a free disseminator of information. But often family members have different styles and comfort levels. Conflict may arise when one family member shares something that another member feels violates his or her privacy. For instance, if mom tells her best friend that her son may be failing calculus, her son (and dad, too) may feel their privacy has been violated. This may hold true even when someone has shared positive information, such as "My daughter got straight As," or, "My son just received an award in Boy Scouts."

It's crucial to understand one another's comfort with sharing information as the college admissions process unfolds. Check with each other frequently about what you may and may not share with friends and family members. Sometimes who does the sharing is also important. It may be perfectly acceptable for your daughter to tell people her SAT scores, but it may trigger World War III if mom or dad reveals this information. Similarly, college visits, grades, early decision applications, regular decision college choices, and financial considerations are all hot-button issues. So a word to the wise: check what topics may be taboo with which family members, and always ask first before revealing any personal data to anyone outside your immediate family—or possibly even siblings.

4. What are the boundaries in your family regarding communication?

This is a corollary of the question asked above concerning the sharing of information. For some families, the boundaries of communication are permeable. It's acceptable to share information with siblings and relatives, as well as nieces, nephews, and cousins. It's the norm for everyone to be in the loop concerning any member of the family. Sometimes there are transgenerational boundaries, namely that there's no problem sharing information with family members of the same generation, but not with the generation older or younger.

In other families, boundaries are restrictive and impermeable, and all information is kept within the nuclear unit. Families that have these more rigid boundaries usually have difficulty sharing information with outsiders who, in their opinion, do not have a need to know. These families believe that they must never air their dirty laundry in public. When college officials or high school guidance counselors request personal data, this makes them feel uncomfortable.

It's crucial to understand one another's comfort with sharing information as the college admissions process unfolds.

5. Is your communication generally more expressive or instrumental?

Those of us who are expressive in our communication style tend to talk about feelings easily. We vent to others and use conversation as an opportunity to work through a problem. Expressive communication often is cathartic, and it generally requires only a good listener for it to be effective.

Those of us who are instrumental communicators often are looking for a way to solve a problem. We want to find ways to change the situation. Merely talking about it does not feel effective. Something needs to be resolved in concrete terms.

Often these two communication styles are seen as gender-related, i.e., women tend to be more expressive and men tend to be more instrumental. Mrs. Thomas complains about how bad her situation is at work. Mr. Thomas suggests she update her resume and start looking for a new job. Mrs. Thomas gets incensed because she did not ask for advice; she just wanted a sympathetic ear. Mr. Thomas is angry that his wife has now attacked him, seemingly out of the blue, when he was just trying to be helpful.

During the college admissions process, both mothers and fathers tend to be more instrumental, while their teenagers tend to be more expressive. Your student may often rail about deadlines, grades, or related concerns. You may want to swoop in to make the situation better. Your own style of communication, coupled with a healthy dose of anxiety, may lead you to offer advice and suggestions. Be aware of what your child is expressing: is he looking for empathy or assistance—or both?

6. Do you look to others to help solve problems or do you prefer to solve them on your own?

Related to the dimension of expressive/instrumental communication patterns is the general approach you may have to problem solving. Do you tend to seek out advice when confronted with a dilemma? Or do you avoid admitting you're struggling and refuse outside assistance?

We often observe this dichotomy when people are lost. What do you do? Do you stop to ask directions? How soon after recognizing you're lost? Or do you resist asking anyone and instead try to figure out where you are by yourself?

Conflict can erupt when a family member is eager to problem solve while another is resistant to any offers of assistance. The demands of the admissions process can lead to a clash of styles if problem-solving styles are not explored ahead of time.

7. How do you express your feelings?

Give some thought to the following: how effective are you in communicating your true feelings?

If an objective observer was trying to determine the emotional content of your communication, could he? For example, do you laugh when talking about something that may be sad? Do you use emotional words to describe how you feel? Are your words consistent with your nonverbal body language and facial expressions?

Before emotions are running high in your household, discuss how comfortable each of you is with sharing feelings. As with all communication, the clearer all family members are about their patterns of behavior and comfort zones, the less likely it is that you will get into conflict.

8. How do you convey differences of opinion?

We suggest you think about how different family members express differences of opinion.

Often, our attitudes and behavior regarding different opinions are shaped by our early experiences. What was modeled by your family of origin? Were differences of opinion challenged? Welcomed? Put down? Respected? Now, in the present, how comfortable are you when someone challenges your opinions?

Raising teenagers is a crash course in learning to tolerate having your ideas challenged. If you say black, you know your teenager will say white. So how can you handle these verbal confrontations? Can you tolerate it? Does it make you angry? Does it shake your own security in your position? Can you use humor to prevent escalation into a major disagreement? Or do you use denial to pretend that nothing is happening in order to avoid conflict?

~During the college admissions process, both mothers and fathers tend to be more instrumental, while their teenagers tend to be more expressive.~

Exploring your own ways of handling differences of opinion is just the first step. How does each family member do so? Can you help your teenager to feel comfortable when you disagree with him? Your teenager may say categorically that he wants to do something, and you may need to disagree wholeheartedly. The issue may be finances, early decision applications, or geographical distance from home. Regardless of the subject, you want to lay the groundwork not only for tolerating differences of opinion, but also for developing strategies for resolving differences and moving forward.

UNRESOLVED FAMILY DYNAMICS

It can be helpful to consider what, if any, unresolved family dynamics may be lurking around the corner. As you are well aware, the admissions process can be long and drawn out, leading to frayed nerves and irritability. This is a recipe for stirring up old feelings about control and who is the perceived winner and loser in family discussions.

The conflict may be between parent and child, between siblings, or between parents. Do you believe you always have to give in to your spouse or partner? Or are you confident that you can usually convince others to do what you want? Have you felt that your teenager has you wrapped around his finger? Or are you confident that you are able to resolve differences to your own satisfaction? Do you ever agree to disagree? And does that resolve matters?

The Saperstein family has avoided direct confrontation about decision making by steering clear of any discussions that could lead to arguments. Tom Saperstein, the college applicant, is used to getting what he wants. He's generally a good student, is well behaved, and does not get into trouble. However, his parents have never tried to set limits on his activities. Now Mr. Saperstein is worried that Tom is not following up on the admissions process as carefully as he should. Mr. Saperstein is not sure if his son has registered to take the SAT, spoken with his guidance counselor, or begun any meaningful aspect of the college search. Mr. Saperstein voices his concern to Mrs. Saperstein, who also tends to be a conflict-avoider. The Sapersteins agree that they need to have a conversation with Tom about their expectations and his expectations, and they need to come up with a process that will enable them to move forward without a fight.

Here are three suggestions for handling difficult discussions:

1.   Rehearse what you actually want to say to your teenager. Although you don't need an actual script, be clear about what you do want to share. Check with your spouse to see if you hold the same views. If not, resolve your differences before you engage your child.

2.   You need to be prepared for several possible responses. You know your child best. Will he get angry? Will he be defensive? Will he capitulate immediately to make peace, but then not follow through? Think through his possible reactions, and be prepared to listen to what he has to say.

3.   Try to anticipate arguments for your position as well as against. As in a debate, you can be firm in your views while maintaining respect for the other people involved and listening to their thoughts.

WHAT'S YOUR COMMUNICATION STYLE AS A COUPLE?

We have discussed how you can assess your individual communication styles, but it's also important for parents to examine their joint communication style. If you as a couple have a good track record of being able to resolve differences, you will probably bring this skill into the college admissions process. You'll be able to exhibit good communication and conflict-resolution skills for your child.

What happens if you don't have such a great track record? We're not suggesting that you can change overnight the patterns of interaction in your family. But we want you to recognize that any family patterns of conflict may be exacerbated during this period.

If there's latent or overt marital discord, it can easily spill over into your interactions with your student. Given the stress and emotionally charged decisions that have to be made, you should be aware of your own vulnerabilities. Make a pact with your significant other to not argue in front of your child. If you disagree with one another about something your child is doing, try to iron out your differences privately. If you can't reach consensus, agree to disagree and neutrally present both positions to your teenager. This is certainly not the time to bring up old grievances or grudges. Your child needs his parents to be the adults.

It's especially important for parents to put aside their own conflicts during the college admissions process. If you continue to fight, not only will you be inflicting more wounds, but there also may be serious repercussions for your child's future. When, where, and how he goes off to college and fares during this transition can have far-reaching ramifications.

OTHER FAMILY SITUATIONS

If you're a single parent, you may have particular struggles with your college-bound teenager. You may not have another adult in your life as a built-in support system to help you deal with adolescent vicissitudes. We strongly encourage you, if you haven't already, to seek out other adults to help during this period. This could be a friend or relative with whom you can try to share the burden of decision making and limit setting. You may also use another adult to help you get perspective on your own communication style.

Parents who are separated or divorced may be at particular risk for bringing in old, negative patterns of communication. Once again, we urge you to work together as a team during this process. If you find yourselves in disagreement, hash it out away from your child. If you need to bring a neutral party into the situation, do so. Step-parents may also help with the process if they have a good relationship with both biological parents. A step-parent can sometimes have a more objective, reasoned assessment of what is occurring.

We're not suggesting that you can change overnight the patterns of interaction in your family. But we want you to recognize that any family patterns of conflict may be exacerbated during the college application process.

In nontraditional families, you may also need to examine different styles of communication and decision making. Who assumes the parental role? Does it shift depending on the issue being discussed? Clearly, whoever is involved in childrearing should be included in college discussions. But it may be necessary to explore the levels of authority that occur in the family structure. Even if the labels in your family are different, the same advice holds true: examine the nature of the communication patterns and discuss how decisions are made. How do you resolve differences, and, ultimately, how can you use this insight to keep conflict at a minimum?

THE CHANGING NATURE OF PARENTAL RELATIONSHIPS

The college search marks the beginning of your family's shift from being a child-focused unit back to a couple-focused one. While you may be reading this book with your oldest child in mind, even if you have more children, the eventual outcome will be an empty nest. You may not yet be completely aware of the sadness or even ambivalence that may accompany working toward sending your teenager off to college.

While this is generally an exciting time, filled with hope and positive expectations for your child, it still is paving the way for him to leave home. Therefore, this is a good opportunity for you and your spouse to communicate honestly with one another about the feelings you may each be experiencing. You may use one another as a mutual support system, not only when things get tough with your teenager, but also when the fear of the unknown gets you down.

You and your spouse should work on spending time with each other, too. Take the time to talk with each other about the admissions process and the numerous emotions it may evoke. Plan dates together so you can feel connected and excited about your own future. This is the time to make especially sure you are not planning to live vicariously through your kids.

FIVE TIPS TO MINIMIZE CONFLICT AND ACHIEVE BETTER COMMUNICATION

Regardless of how well or poorly your family communicates with one another now, there's always room for improvement. The better the quality of family interaction and communication, the less chance there will be for miscommunication and conflict. To improve your family's shared experiences, we suggest the following:

1. Select a day and time to have a family discussion. Try to do so on a regular basis. Come together and share good things that are happening with each family member.

2. Practice actively listening without responding until the other family member cedes the floor. Mirror back what the other person has said, "What I hear you saying is . . ."

3.   Try to eat more meals together as a family. Studies consistently show that students have fewer problems when families eat together regularly.

4.   Have each family member make a list of ongoing priorities for the college search. Compare lists on a regular basis. Incorporate the priorities into one document that's then available for everyone to use and amend at future get-togethers.

5.   Engage in an activity that the entire family enjoys at least once every few weeks. Some suggestions include:

▶   Watching a movie that everyone likes.
▶   Planning and cooking a meal together.
▶   Taking a walk through your neighborhood.
▶   Attending as many of your student's activities (sports, drama, etc.) as he will let you.
▶   Organizing a trip together as a family, which could be a college campus visit. Let each family member get to do at least one thing he wants to do.
▶   Planning an outing that everyone enjoys, such as ice-skating or a picnic.

8

Family Member Responsibilities

If you only remember one thing from this chapter, remember the following: as a parent, you must keep careful track of admissions deadlines. We understand the need for student responsibility—and we'll be talking about that after we address parental responsibility—but one of your most important tasks is to maintain the family calendar as it relates to college admissions timelines.

PARENTAL RESPONSIBILITIES

Your teenager has a great deal on her plate. She has to manage school and extracurricular activities, while coping with the usual social demands and sleep deprivation of high school students. Attention to the admissions schedule is probably not a priority. Therefore, keeping your child on track is essential. We recommend regularly going over to-do lists as a family. This way everyone knows what he or she is expected to do.

We suggest that you review the family calendar, including college-related tasks, after dinner every Sunday night. Your student can explain the projects, academic work, and other activities she has during the following week. You can discuss upcoming admissions deadlines and help her weave the necessary admissions preparation into her schedule and possibly yours as well.

It's unlikely that your high school student will come to you and say, "Mom, I don't really have enough to do this week. Can I make sure that I sign up for the SAT or ACT with enough time so that we don't have to pay a late fee?"

As the grown-up, you bear the responsibility of keeping your child on track. Be aware of deadlines for applications, standardized tests, and summer programs. For each of these areas, be sure to have your teenager do some of the preparatory work.

However, avoid making this your college application process rather than your child's. Don't fall into the trap of doing all of the college-related work yourself. When you have your weekly family scheduling meeting, you and your child should review the college admissions to-do list, and clearly assign tasks and dates by which these tasks need to be completed.

Here is a list of some important deadlines as well as possible consequences of failing to meet them. Use this as a starting-off point in discussions with your teenager. The consequences should not be posed as threats. Rather, they are the natural outcomes. You also must gauge your willingness to allow these consequences to occur. You need to determine if you'll allow your child to potentially harm her college admissions chances, or, if and when you may have to step in.

1.   **SAT or ACT registration:** There are typically six or seven test dates during each academic year. Generally, registration deadlines are one to two months before the test.

Possible consequences:

▶   Your student may be placed at a test location far from home or your local high school.

▶   Your teenager may not have enough time during the school year to take the SAT more than once (if she doesn't do well the first time).

▶   Your child may not have enough time to take up to three SAT Subject Tests.

▶   Other necessary activities may interfere with later test dates (e.g., a state championship game, year-end school social, or family event such as a wedding).

2.   **College visits:** Plan your schedule to allow several college tours and
     campus visits.

Possible consequences:

▶   If you wait too long, you may have to schedule your visits when there
    are no students on campus. This will dramatically alter the feel of the
    school.
▶   You may end up visiting campuses during a season of the year when
    the weather is especially hot or cold, and it might not be an accurate
    reflection of the campus's "climate" during the academic year.
▶   If you run out of time and apply to schools sight unseen, your student is
    more likely to have a problem determining which school is the best fit.

3.   **Community service hours:** Many high schools now require a certain
     number of community service hours to be completed before graduation.

Possible consequences:

▶   If your student waits too long, she may not be able to graduate on time.
▶   If your student waits too long, the requirement may interfere with
    other plans, activities, or academic demands.

4.   **Summer programs or internships:** Encourage your student to make
     her summer plans early so she potentially has more options to choose
     from. It's never too early to prompt your teenager to use the summer
     to explore her interests and
     pursue activities that include   ∼Encourage your student to
     these interests.   make her summer plans early so
                                           she potentially has more options
Possible consequences: to choose from.∼

▶   If your student waits too long
    to look for internship possibilities, she may not find any.
▶   If your student waits too long, she may not find a program that taps
    her passion or interest. For example, while she may find a job as a

camp counselor, she may not get the job as the science educator at a summer program that would have allowed her to develop further her interests in science and teaching.

5.   **Letters of recommendation:** Your student will probably need two letters of recommendation from teachers for each college application.

Possible consequences:

▸   If your student waits until her senior year to ask teachers to write her recommendations, many teachers may have already committed to other students and may turn her down. This can happen even if your student has an excellent relationship with a teacher.

▸   If your student doesn't ask her teacher for a recommendation in a timely fashion and get the necessary paperwork to her, the teacher may decline to write the letter because of her own time constraints.

Key Parental Responsibilities:

1.   Keep track of deadlines.
2.   Have regular conversations about what needs to be done, by what date, and by whom.
3.   Make travel arrangements for campus visits, including airline, train, bus, hotel, and car rental reservations. Block out your calendar and your student's calendar as early as possible. Advance planning will help you secure more convenient reservations and campus appointments.
4.   Be aware of financial concerns. How much is your family able and willing to spend?
5.   Familiarize yourself with the U.S. Department of Education's Free Application for Federal Student Aid and the College Scholarship Service Profile Form, and complete them as soon as you can in order to receive financial aid packages as early as possible.

CAMPUS VISITS

One of the more important tasks for parents is to facilitate visits to college campuses.

Encourage your student to explore a wide variety of colleges before deciding on specifics. Have her look at large, medium, and small schools. Often students have one particular type of school in mind—even though they have never explored any other kinds. Later, you will want to help your child focus on narrowing her choices, but for now, the name of the game is exploration.

Decide as a family when to begin visiting colleges and how many trips you may want to take over the next year or two. Generally, tenth grade is a good time to begin. Pick a few colleges near your home and plan to take a tour and attend an information session. Even if these colleges prove not to be ideal for your child, at least you will have begun the process in your child's mind. She will see that you are serious—and she will physically see some universities.

We know that her academic interests are likely to change, but visiting college campuses can inspire her to look beyond the here-and-now of high school. If she is inspired and enthusiastic, getting her to do the more mundane tasks related to college admissions will be easier for all of you.

At this stage, you should defer serious conversations with your teenager about the applications themselves. The goal now is to use the process of visiting colleges to get her excited about the prospect of attending college. The more you can do to make this process fun, the better.

⌒We know that her academic interests are likely to change, but visiting college campuses can inspire her to look beyond the here-and-now of high school.⌒

In terms of scheduling visits, often the problem rests more with your calendar than with your child's level of enthusiasm. Make sure that you make time to visit schools. There's almost never a convenient time to get away from work or household responsibilities. But you must do so if you want your child to feel that college is not some distant idea. The visits also will help you to see firsthand some of the changes that have taken place on campuses in the past twenty to thirty years.

Parents regularly report that they enjoy the trips to colleges. Just a few hours in a car can give a parent the time to learn about the goings-on in her daughter's life (as opposed to "How was school today, Sarah?" "Fine."), and teenagers usually are much more willing to talk when they're sitting in an automobile.

During college visits, let your student react to the colleges before you share your own opinions. Your child knows that you'll have an opinion, but whatever you do, don't express your thoughts until after your child has thoroughly discussed the pros and cons of a school in her own words. She needs to feel that she can respond honestly to her own feelings and impressions of the different schools.

One of the appealing aspects of college for many high school students is the feeling that they will soon be on their own. They want to go to their own college and have their own college experiences. Therefore, you want to be very cautious about sharing your own college experiences with your child unless she specifically asks. Try to avoid a running comparison between your alma mater and the colleges you are visiting.

Generally, students are interested in hearing about your college experiences and your views about college only if these views correspond with their own. This is one reason why you should let your child react first. Even if you develop a visceral dislike for a particular school, keep that opinion to yourself initially. There will be plenty of time to discuss various colleges over the next year or two.

STUDENT RESPONSIBILITIES

We encourage you to sit down with your teenager and explain that everyone in the family has responsibilities in the college admissions process and that she is expected to handle her share. Yes, you should do your part as a parent, but it's your student who will be attending college. We urge you to help her clearly understand that she has responsibilities to fulfill—and that these are critical. If she doesn't do her part, she will probably not be pleased with the final results.

We suggest that you prepare a written list and then speak with your child about her key responsibilities.

Ten Key Student Responsibilities:

1.   Take time to think about your interests and goals for college.

2.   Take time to think about your possible career interests.

3.   Take time to think about different features of a college: setting (urban, rural, suburban), location (East, West, Midwest, South, etc.), size, religious affiliation, single-sex vs. coeducational, liberal arts or pre-professional, etc.

4.   Conduct searches to explore matches for (1), (2), and (3).

5.   Research colleges online.

6.   Submit forms for tests, including the SATs.

7.   Request letters of recommendation from teachers and others.

8.   Write college application essays.

9.   Request that your high school transcript be sent to each college to which you are applying.

10.   Make reservations for campus interviews and college information sessions and tours. (Okay, your parents can help with this one if they really want to.)

You and your child should consider a broad array of college options. Do not just follow what your neighbors and classmates do. By looking beyond the traditional schools that your neighbors and friends usually consider, you will be helping your child to expand her horizons. There's no better way to achieve this than to consider colleges that were initially unfamiliar to you.

But how are you supposed to consider schools that you don't know about in the first place? One way is to attend as many college fairs as you can—both with and without your teenager. If your daughter has a math test tomorrow and needs to study for it, then we recommend that you go to the college fair by yourself. Don't worry: you won't be the only parent in attendance.

Your student's high school guidance counselor should be able to give you the schedule of fairs in your area. They usually are held in schools, fairgrounds, and hotels and often involve fifty to one hundred college representatives who sit behind tables and answer questions about their particular colleges. Be prepared to ask specific questions related to your child's academic interests, course offerings, and extracurricular life on campus.

Your student can follow up on the college fair by reading the brochures provided and by visiting the colleges' websites. Explain to her that she should not expect a college to advertise its weaknesses, but that a great deal of information can be gleaned by examining what a college chooses to emphasize. Does it choose to showcase its social life (lots of pictures of students at parties and sporting events), or does it instead emphasize its academic life (lots of pictures of students studying in the library)? How does a college describe its location? Most high school students can find New York and Boston on a map—but where is Kalamazoo, Michigan? It's not twenty hours from Chicago, but it's not a commutable distance either. Is a college putting a more positive spin on available social opportunities than is realistic? How truthfully a college describes its location is usually a good indicator of the trustworthiness of the rest of the college's marketing materials.

After you and your child have looked at a number of brochures and websites—and come to some tentative agreement about possible preferences—you should begin planning visits to various campuses. Let your son or daughter make the first suggestion of where to visit. We have found that students who make the initial choices—with parental input afterward, of course—are much more engaged in the actual campus visits.

Emphasize to your teenager that she needs to be actively involved in these campus visits. Each one costs time and money, both of which are precious commodities for most families. Explain to your student that it is she who may be attending this college, and that she should do her best to learn as much from the visit as she can. Kids will be kids, so don't worry if your daughter's first comment concerns the attractiveness of students on campus. After a few sentences about her potential social life, encourage her to share with you her other impressions of the college.

We suggest that your student make lists of her interests and goals—and that you as the parent make sure that the lists actually get done. Explain to your teenager that her lists of interests are just drafts, but that they will help her figure out if particular colleges might be able to satisfy these interests. You as the parent can make lists also, but again we have found that student-generated lists tend to motivate students more than lists drawn up by their parents.

We encourage you to speak with your child about her short- and long-term goals. What does she hope to get from her college experience? Where does she see herself in five or ten years? Warning: it's likely that your teenager will be unable or unwilling to answer these questions directly. Ask them anyway. Even if she won't discuss them with you, she might talk about them with her friends later. Then you will have done your job; you will have helped her begin to think seriously about her future.

The same holds true for discussions about learning styles and university environments. Just by raising the issues in a serious way, you contribute to your child's college search. By helping her think about the ways in which she learns best, you are encouraging her to think about the types of colleges that emphasize her style of learning.

Ask your child to explain to either you or her friends how she learns best. Does she thrive in small classes with lots

~We suggest that your student make lists of her interests and goals—and that you as the parent make sure that the lists actually get done.~

of individual attention—or does she do better with the anonymity that large educational settings allow? If you explore learning styles first, you will likely find that discussions about university environments flow more smoothly.

Try to create an environment in which you, your spouse, and your child can openly and honestly discuss each other's needs and wants. It's quite common for spouses to disagree about the type of university that they think will best serve their child—not to mention that most teenagers look at the world differently from their parents.

Encourage your teenager to leave plenty of time for her college essays. Students regularly say that "I've finished everything on my college applications except for the essays." That's the equivalent of asking, "How else was the play, Mrs. Lincoln?"

Essays are crucial elements of many college applications. They help admissions officers decide which students to accept and which to deny. But perhaps even more importantly, although students don't always see it this way, essays enable them to clarify their thinking about their future college experience.

School or Third-Party Responsibilities:

There are a number of application-related items for which neither you nor your child are directly responsible—even though they have a direct impact on your child's applications. You need to be aware of all relevant deadlines and requests, including the actions that others need to complete on your behalf:

1.   Your student's high school, as part of the admissions process, must send out her official transcript to each college.
2.   The high school guidance counselor needs to write and complete your student's school recommendation letter.
3.   The teachers who will be writing letters of recommendation must complete and send them by the due dates.
4.   The College Board or ACT must send scores to the colleges specified by your child.

FINANCIAL CONSIDERATIONS

One of the most delicate areas of the college search and admissions process is money. Often families don't feel comfortable explaining to their student the financial limits that are going to be necessary.

We urge you to sit down with your teenager, explain that you are excited about her college prospects, discuss the cost of various colleges, and walk her through different ways to pay for school.

There are some who believe that financing a child's education is solely a parental responsibility, while others believe that the child should bear the full cost. Most Americans believe that college is a joint venture between students and parents. We agree, so we believe that you should help your student secure the loans necessary for her college education, if these become necessary.

We suggest that you begin the discussion with your teenager about actual college costs. Often, teenagers are unable to comprehend costs that can easily exceed $100,000. Even more frequently, they don't understand the consequences of incurring significant debt. Use a loan calculator to show your student that each $7,500 borrowed means that she will be responsible for paying approximately $100 per month for ten years. Change the amount borrowed or the loan rate so that your child can see how they affect repayment.

Loans can have a real impact on students' post-college career choices, so we urge you to go over independent living costs with your teenager. What are the rents like in the areas where she hopes to live after college? By showing her the costs of actual living situations, you will help her understand how debt may have an impact on some of her future choices. At the very least, you will begin to see her comfort level as it relates to different levels of debt.

You may want to discuss the starting salaries of various post-college jobs with your teenager. Take a look at what your child may earn for the first few years after college and what she will be able to afford with different loan burdens.

A further consideration is the graduation rate. There has been a trend in recent years for students to take longer to graduate. Many education statistics now use six years as the yardstick for measuring college graduation rates. If there's a strong likelihood that your child will attend a graduate or professional school, you may need to factor in the loans necessary to continue her education. Try to be realistic not only about what you can afford, but also about what each of you is willing to sacrifice in the future to pay off student loans.

As a parent, it's easy to feel awkward about money when you compare yourself with friends or neighbors. Let's say that an expensive private university has become very popular in your area. If so, there's a reasonable chance that your child will want to at least explore that school. Imagine that you visit the campus. Your daughter says, "Mom, this is it! I found my perfect school." On one hand, you're happy that your child has found a school that offers her what she believes she wants. But then you check your savings account and financial obligations, and you realize that you would be $20,000 short per year if your child attended this college.

Speak honestly and clearly with your teenager. If you believe that you cannot afford what your student wants, we suggest you say so. This will probably lead to a discussion about loans. How much debt are you (and your child) comfortable incurring? Again, refer to the loan calculator and the approximate rent costs. Go over the monthly expenses that will need to be paid before nights out on the town, ski vacations, and dates. We are not recommending that you refuse to take out loans but that you understand the ramifications. If your child's dream school is available only through loans, and you and your child determine that the debt load will be manageable, then, by all means, seriously consider that college.

If you don't want to incur debt to pay for a particular college—or if you don't believe that a particular college is worth its tuition—then you should share this with your teenager. Some students will simply accept your statement, while others will ask you to explain why you feel this way. An open discussion as a family can bring everyone together and help each of you understand the way the others think.

9

Teamwork Every Step of the Way

While generational battles between children and parents almost always take place, this does not mean that you cannot, or should not, try to understand the different ways in which you and your child view the world. Today's parents went to school surrounded by current events, pop icons, and technology vastly different than those their children encounter. It's useful to explore these differences, as well as any similarities, in order to develop a shared language with your child.

You also see the world differently because you are at different stages of life. The first order of business is to recognize the legitimacy of your teenager's concerns. For example, your son will probably consider his social life a higher priority than you do. He may be interested in attending a large university with a highly regarded sports program and robust campus party scene, while you may prefer smaller, more intimate schools.

HELPING YOUR TEENAGER FIND HIS OWN ROAD

A good way to start to reconcile possible child-parent differences is to establish a dialogue. You both need to be able to answer this question: what do you hope your child gets from his college experience? Frequently, key areas of disagreement center on the size of the school, the location, distance from home, and whether or not your child wants to apply to your alma mater. Additionally, differences may arise regarding the ranking and nature of the college. Your child may say he wants a more laid-back school, while you or your spouse may be pushing for the most competitive school to which he may be able to gain admission. You may also find yourself disagreeing with your daughter's expressed academic area of interest. You may have expected her to be pre-med, but she may have a different plan in mind.

If you find yourself in the midst of these differences in outlooks and opinions, our advice is to do nothing at first. Ask your teenager about the types of educational institutions that seem to be attracting him. Let him talk about his thoughts—without expressing your own. Many of his notions may be just that—uncensored ideas that he may be sending up as trial balloons. There will be ample opportunities later for you to express your opinions and ideas. If you come on too strong at the beginning, you will quash any potential for a real meeting of the minds later on.

IS NOW THE TIME FOR YOUR CHILD TO GO TO COLLEGE?

Over the course of raising your child, you will have gotten to know his study habits, grades, and overall level of maturity. We urge you to reflect on this history and think about how you would feel if your child did not go to college immediately after high school. Would you worry that he would never go back to school? Has this option already come up? If so, who brought it up in the first place? Have you spoken with your spouse about a possible gap in your child's education? We urge you to have this discussion. You, your spouse, and your child may all have disparate views, both emotional and strategic, on taking time off before entering college.

The college admissions process will help you to assess whether your child is actually ready to go to college. You will be able to see how he handles deadlines. How mature is he? Is he picking colleges because of what girls look like on campus? Is he taking the process seriously? Is he researching universities and taking care of his college-related administrative responsibilities?

Before you arrive at the conclusion that it may be a good idea for your son or daughter to take some time off to mature and develop a stronger college application, think about whether it actually makes sense for your child to take an academic break. How will the time be used? What will your teenager be accomplishing? Will he be doing community service, taking art classes, or engaging in other positive experiences—or does he want to relax for a year?

We're supportive of gap-year programs, sometimes even for two years, but only if your student is willing to have educational experiences rather than purely social ones. Not everyone agrees, though, that gap years are a good idea. Many parents believe that if students take time off, they'll never go back to school. We believe that for the motivated but burnt-out or immature child, gap-year options are good to explore.

Can taking time off improve your student's chances of getting into college? In a word, yes. A year helps students mature, which almost always comes through in the actual college choices as well as in interviews. Having a year or more of interesting experiences usually makes it easier to have something to write about in an application essay.

HELPING YOUR CHILD EXPLORE ACADEMIC INTERESTS

Throughout your child's education, whenever he has choices, encourage him to study what he likes. Encourage him to talk about these subjects with you. Look for openings in conversations that will enable you to help him explore beyond what he has learned in the classroom. One suggestion is for you to read books from the library or bookstore so that you can be reasonably up-to-date on these subjects as well. Encourage your child to delve into both the academic elements as well as practical activities that may relate to his interests.

But don't push so much as to discourage your child from exploring other fields. Demonstrate sincere interest in the subject matter. At the same time, make sure you don't take over his interests—and definitely don't try to become more of an authority than he is.

How strongly should you push? If your teenager thinks about his academic areas of interest on his own, outside of school, then you might not have to push too hard. The student who doesn't spend hours thinking about his academic interests is the one who most needs the encouragement.

How should you approach this subject? We suggest that you try to make majors and careers real for your child. For example, if you have friends or colleagues who know something about a particular field, or who work in it, invite them over for dinner. Encourage them to discuss age-appropriate jobs and volunteer opportunities that can help your teenager clarify his interests. Then let your friend or colleague engage your child in conversation—without you in the room.

You'll likely have an opinion about your child's areas of interest. Try not to show your biases or preconceived notions about various academic subjects. Let your child explain his views of his fields of knowledge or prospective careers. His ideas may sound unrealistic to you, but really listen to what he has to say. It's okay for your child to use you as a sounding board.

~Encourage your child to delve into both the academic elements as well as practical activities that may relate to his interests.~

Just because one day your child announces he wants to be a full-time ballroom dance instructor doesn't mean he'll continue to want to focus on this occupation. However, if you criticize your child's interests or career ideas too quickly, he may not come back to speak with you about them again.

This is easier said than done. You may cringe when your child expresses interest in doing something that has no realistic prospect for making a decent living. But for the moment, keep these thoughts to yourself.

Help your child understand his course options at college. Encourage him to look through course catalogs, not just admissions materials. Try to follow the various course sequences within different academic departments. This preview often will help you determine how serious your student could be about a particular major.

Additionally, avoid pushing a particular career. Focus instead on the possible practical applications of his interests. This is when summer programs can be invaluable in helping students match interests with possible future career options. Keep in mind that different roads can lead to the same destination. For example, if your student believes he may want to be a lawyer, he can major in any area he would like while in college.

HOW TO DISCUSS MAJOR ISSUES IN COLLEGE SELECTION WITH YOUR CHILD

The more important the issue, the more care that should go into discussing it. This is especially true when your child might feel that you are judging him. Be sure to show respect for him as an individual. Do so by trying to follow his lead. If he's interested in a school because of the social atmosphere, proximity to cultural institutions, or perceptions of the political mood on campus, let him explore these avenues.

In the same way that it's highly unlikely that you'll be able to convince him that broccoli is tastier than chocolate cake, it's also unlikely that you'll be able to convince him to focus exclusively on the academic life of his possible future college. Nevertheless, encourage your child to articulate his interests as clearly as possible.

Think of yourself more as an inquiring reporter than as an advice-giving adult. Your child may not be able to convince you of his position, but you can at least engage in a mature conversation with him. You may even debate the merits of his choices. Whatever you may think about his arguments, you always need to remember that this is his college experience you are exploring.

Families often hotly debate the size of the student body. Often parents are concerned that their child won't be able to get the individualized attention they believe she needs. Students, on the other hand, frequently are focused on their social lives and are looking for larger universities with what they perceive to be greater opportunities for social interactions and more overall excitement. Of course, there are exceptions to every rule, and your teenager may or may not fit this description. In either case, we urge you to sit down and discuss the pros and cons of school size with your child.

> ～The more important the issue, the more care that should go into discussing it. This is especially true when your child might feel that you are judging him.～

If you're unable to resolve the issue of size of the student body with your child, then you'll need to agree to disagree and then include both large and small schools on the initial college list—leaving the decision about where to apply for a later date. This is where campus visits will play a crucial role in the college decision-making process. You and your child may disagree about any number of aspects of different schools, but until you visit several campuses, your discussions will all be theoretical. Once you have the firsthand experience of exploring a number of institutions, you will all be in a better position to evaluate where your child will ultimately feel comfortable.

The most discussed cultural issue that can lead to generational conflict is the concern about sexual attitudes and activity on college campuses. College campuses generally are more lenient about sexual relationships, both heterosexual and homosexual, than most parents are in their homes. College environments are also much more tolerant than when some family members attended college. It wasn't that long ago when virtually all residence halls were single-sex and contact with members of the opposite sex in a dormitory was controlled. Students had to sign in and out, and they had to be back in their dormitories by a certain time.

The question of single-sex versus coed education brings up some difficult issues for families of high school girls. Yes, there are still a handful of single-sex male colleges, but not very many. While fewer than 10 percent of U.S. high school girls are willing to consider women's colleges, it often seems as if almost 100 percent of their fathers are particularly interested in these fifty-four women-only institutions.

> ∼The most discussed cultural issue that can lead to generational conflict is the concern about sexual attitudes and activity on college campuses.∼

There is no delicate way to bridge this gap, but our advice is for mothers to take the lead in moderating these family discussions. Try to rationally explore the pros and cons of women's colleges. Listen to both sides and then examine other aspects of college aside from social life. What is the overall academic quality? Does the college have the courses your daughter is interested in? What about location? What about developing leadership skills?

Religiosity and religious affiliation can be sensitive issues for many families. Students and parents do not always completely agree about the role of religion in their lives. One member of your family may be more religious than the others and may be more interested in the spiritual life on various campuses. Again, conversation is the only way to move forward. It might be that the less-religious party is willing to explore campuses that offer, but don't require, more religious involvement. Parents may be able to accept that religious experiences are readily available at certain colleges, even if they recognize that their son or daughter may not choose to participate.

For some families, though, religion may be so central that they need to consider the affiliation of the school. Parents may be willing to allow their child to leave home only if he attends a religiously affiliated college. Some teenagers don't feel limited by this restriction. For others, it may be the deal breaker. A frank family discussion is vital. Pros and cons need to be addressed, as well as parental fears regarding a child's exposure to new influences. Each family should try to resolve this in a manner that is mutually respectful and realistic.

Distance from home is also a sensitive issue in college admissions. Often parents want their children to be within a few hours' drive from home, while this is a less-than-unanimous position among high school students. High school students are at the age at which they want to seek out new things—and this often includes wanting to explore new places as well.

We urge you to at least permit your child to look into out-of-town universities. If you don't immediately forbid him from traveling a certain distance from home, he'll often retreat later, back to the familiar. When he realizes that travel is not always hassle-free, and that it's inconvenient to transport dirty clothes through multiple airports, he may come to understand by himself that being closer to home is not so bad.

BUMPS ON THE ROAD

Some students simply don't excel in academics. It's unreasonable to expect your child to achieve beyond his ability level. For instance, it would be unrealistic to assume that with practice, we could all participate in the next Olympics. It may be an ongoing struggle to determine if your child is working to his potential or not.

Be aware that your child may have developed fears related to his academic progress. Some teenagers are actually afraid of success. They're afraid that others might perceive them in a different light. They may have developed a vested interest in having others, and themselves, view them as an average student. They may feel that it's easier to be in the middle of the pack than to stand out, even if it's in a positive way.

Teenagers can have a fear of failure, too, so they avoid putting in 100 percent effort. If they don't try and later fail, they can blame lack of effort.

They would have been able to succeed if only they had tried harder. But if they try their hardest and still fail, this may threaten their self-esteem.

Parents and children often disagree about the need for any outside intervention. Many students have the fantasy that once they graduate from high school, they can be fully functioning independent adults who don't need help from anyone. You should be firm but supportive while insisting that your child needs to receive whatever professional support is necessary to overcome the bumps ahead. Be clear that you are not trying to keep him a child. Rather, you want to pass on the baton so that he can learn to take care of himself.

It can be difficult for teenagers to accept that they have limitations. Don't expect this to be a one-time discussion. You may have to revisit your child's fears time and again over the course of the admissions process. You can be empathetic about how hard it is for anyone to look at their own vulnerabilities. But failing to have these discussions about limitations can lead to much bigger problems later. Try to underscore the positive aspects of your teenager's taking charge of his own needs. Emphasize that it's a sign of maturity to accept personal liabilities, as well as personal strengths.

COMMON SCENARIOS THAT LEAD TO ARGUMENTS— AND WHAT TO DO ABOUT THEM

▶ "I'll finish my social studies project at the end-of-the-semester party. My two best friends will be there; we'll discuss it then."

Often collaboration is the key to success, but we encourage you to suggest that serious learning usually takes place best in an environment conducive to thinking, listening, and writing. Be supportive of your student's engaging in a positive social life, but try to help him understand that it's usually a good idea to separate his school responsibilities from his social activities. The better this is established before your child's departure for college, the easier his transition to college will be.

▶ "I just don't have any time to visit colleges this semester."

If need be, you must insist that your son miss a football practice or theater rehearsal. College visits should not be optional. As we've recommended, try to arrange these visits in advance so they can be locked into your schedules. No matter how good your planning may be, though, your child still may end up having to miss some activities in order to fit in campus visits. If that's the case, use the trade-off as a learning experience for the whole family. The life lesson is that no one can do everything all the time. What you can work on here, as a family, is discussing what you're willing to give up and in what order. For example, it may be better to miss a cross-country practice than the school play.

▶ "I finished everything but the essay."

This announcement may call for a family discussion in which timelines are examined and deadlines set. You need to impress upon your child the need for timeliness. You can empathize that writing college application essays can be challenging, demanding, and even boring, but he still needs to do it. Encourage your teenager to think seriously about his future while working on his essays. Remind him that life planning is difficult for everyone and that it's no surprise that he might be thinking about various ways to approach his essays.

▶ "My husband just can't accept that our daughter deserves anything less than Harvard or Yale. He won't make time to explore more realistic possibilities."

You need to explain to your spouse that even the very best students don't have a good chance of being admitted to Ivy League schools. You should insist on making other campus trips—and, if necessary, plan to travel alone with your child to visit other universities. The sooner everyone in the family develops a realistic understanding of your child's chances of being accepted at various colleges, the smoother the admissions process will go.

10

Making a Match

Adolescents come in all shapes and sizes. Their worldviews and ambitions vary dramatically. As a parent, you know that what works with one of your children may not necessarily work with another. Just as you have to assess what childrearing techniques work best for each child, so too must you assess how your child's personality will mesh with different colleges.

EXPLORING SIX KEY DIMENSIONS OF YOUR CHILD'S PERSONALITY

Each teenager is unique and our task as parents is to foster our children's uniqueness. The college community that may be right for your neighbor or one of your other children may not be right for this particular adolescent. Examining your child's special qualities, as well as her particular emotional, educational, and personality needs, can be exciting as well as challenging.

There are over 4,000 colleges and universities in the United States and Canada. Like adolescents, colleges and universities come in all shapes and sizes. There's no secret formula for arriving at the best-fit college for your teenager. It would be much easier if you could just plug in numbers and out would come a solution: for example, (A)cademics + (B)est standardized test scores + (C)ommunity service + (D)esire to attend a specific school = Perfect College Fit. But that's only wishful thinking. So the challenge is to understand all the assets (and any liabilities) your adolescent brings to the admissions process.

A good college match for your child may be different from what worked for you. Your alma mater may be a wonderful choice for your teenager, or it may be absolutely the wrong place for your child to flourish. You may have always regretted not having had the Pac-10 university experience and wish your child could have it. But perhaps he or she would thrive in a different college environment.

To help you and your student connect the dots between what she wants from college and where she can best find it, we have provided a framework to explore the question of what makes your child unique. If your child develops a greater sense of self-awareness, she will be better equipped to make informed, positive decisions about college.

Think about this chapter as an opportunity to explore your adolescent's way of relating to the world. We've selected six key dimensions that examine teen personalities and attitudes, each on a separate continuum. We suggest placement on this continuum as an exercise you can do individually, as well as a family activity in which you also explore how you view one another. Do both you and your spouse come up with the same assessment of your child's personality? Does your child have a totally different view of herself than you do?

Use these facets of your child's personality as starting points for discussion. Exploring "who your child really is" will help you focus the college search. In addition to fostering a positive family discussion, this exercise can help to develop a composite picture of the type of college that will best suit your teenager. You can also use this exploration as a follow-up to an Internet search, college catalog examination, or meeting with your child's college counselor.

RISK TAKER<————————————————>RISK AVERSE/CAUTIOUS

Suzie is an active, outgoing seventeen-year-old who loves adventure. She has attended sleepaway camp since she was eight years old. She recently returned from a trip to Central America, where she participated in a community service project. She's most comfortable when she's trying something new, especially if it involves a certain level of risk. As a child, Suzie loved roller coasters and challenging herself to try daring new activities. Her love of risks even spilled into her academic work. She chose to take the most challenging courses, including AP classes as soon as they were offered in her school. Suzie is most comfortable when she's in novel or challenging situations. She drove her parents crazy for months before she passed her driver's license test. She craved the freedom to drive whenever and wherever she wanted to go. She and her parents still battle about her use of the car.

Now let's look at Jim. He has always felt most comfortable in familiar surroundings. He has a set of close friends with whom he feels most secure and at ease. He avoids new situations, especially if they involve much physical or emotional risk. Jim takes a long time to adjust to each new school year, having spent much of the previous year getting used to his teachers and courses. He plays the same musical instrument he started in elementary school, and he's reluctant to take up new activities or hobbies. He's reluctant to put himself in any situation in which he may fail. He drives a car only when necessary, as he still feels insecure behind the wheel. He avoids talking to his parents about college because he's anxious about the adjustments he'll have to make upon leaving high school. In his heart, he's not sure he even wants to attend a college away from home.

~To help you and your student connect the dots between what she wants from college and where she can best find it, we have provided a framework to explore the question of what makes your child unique.~

Jim and Suzie are at either end of the risk-taking spectrum. Clearly, to make a good choice of colleges to consider, it's helpful to think about where your child falls. Some of the practical considerations include:

- the college's distance from your home,
- the size of the college or university,
- how diverse or homogeneous the college's student population is,
- how similar or different the college's student population is from your child,
- how traditional or nontraditional the college is, and,
- how much the college pushes, both explicitly—such as the required curriculum—and implicitly, to stretch its students. Does the college

seek out the student who is more eager for challenge and exploration or does the college encourage a more traditional model of higher education?

Other specifics to consider include residence halls and student life. Is your child going to be comfortable in a coed dorm? Is there pressure to join fraternities and sororities? Is there enough room for the risk taker to stretch socially, intellectually, and behaviorally? Academically, does the college require taking courses in many areas, including subjects that have never been a strong suit for your teenager? Is there an effective advisor or mentor program, or are students expected to be on their own right from the start?

These questions and an understanding of your child's personality characteristics will enable you to help select schools to consider that will be a good fit.

The following are examples of questions that will help you gather more information regarding your student's attitudes toward risk taking. Feel free to make up and ask your own questions as well.

Questions to ask your teenager:

▶ Have you been to sleepaway camp?
▶ Do you choose the hardest courses offered in your high school?
▶ Do you enjoy trying new activities?

Questions to ask regarding college choices:

▶ How similar is the college's student body to your high school?
▶ How traditional is the required curriculum?

Family discussion questions:

▶ What is your favorite activity at an amusement park?
▶ When you go on vacation, how do you like to spend your time?
▶ What is your favorite form of transportation? Why?
▶ If you could be anyone from history, who would you choose?

KNOWING YOUR PASSION<——>SEEKING YOUR PASSION

Many young people fall somewhere in between these two end points. Adolescence is a period of trial and error. Teenagers are free to explore possible passions, and high school is often an ideal time to do so. Russell may discover that, while he's an excellent swimmer and considers the sport his passion for the moment, he's not sure how to translate it into a career. Could he be a swim coach? Or should he look for an entirely different interest to pursue as a career? While Robin is extremely artistic, and she designs all the sets for the high school plays, does she want to make art or set design her career goal?

Each family member should also examine his or her passion. What do you enjoy doing more than anything else? Did you make a career out of your passion? Is it a vocation or an avocation? What about your child? Can she pursue her passion as a career? Or will it be a hobby? Did you do what your father or mother did? Did you do what your parents did not want you to do? In retrospect, did you follow your passion?

Ultimately, your teenager's understanding of her passion or the search for her passion can be important in selecting a college that's a good fit. If your child knows without a doubt what career path she wishes to follow, then a school with a particular pre-professional program or a specific program in one field of interest may be a good path to explore. On the other hand, if she doesn't know what she is looking for professionally, a college that encourages exploration of various paths is a good place to start.

Some students know from an early age what they want to do when they grow up. After the first assertions of wanting to be a ballet dancer, a firefighter, a teacher, an astronaut, or a professional baseball player, children start to envision themselves in different roles. Some teenagers develop a passion even before they enter high school, and they are certain of what they want to pursue as a career.

Jack might be such a student. He has always loved the movies. He was fascinated for years by his parents' picture taking, and he got his first camera at an early age. Jack took still photos, but he didn't find this sufficiently gratifying. So he moved on to video. He's been making home movies since middle school, and he knows this is what he wants as a career. Jack spends all of his time, when not in school, pursuing his dream of entering the film industry.

He's not sure if he wants to edit, direct, or produce movies, but Jack has set his sights on being involved in some way with filmmaking. Jack is someone who knows his passion and will follow it to college. He'll make a school selection based, in large part, on where he can get the best education to prepare him for his intended career.

Jill, on the other hand, has not yet discovered her passion. She spends most of her time doing schoolwork, socializing with friends, and surfing the Internet. She has tried sports, music, and other extracurricular activities, but nothing has grabbed her interest. Jill views college as a place to find her passion. When asked, she's quite comfortable responding that she has no idea what she wants to do when she graduates from college. She plans to put "undecided" as her intended major on her college applications. Jill has the expectation that college will be the place to determine her interests and develop her career goals.

Once again, we have two students who represent polar opposites on a personality dimension.

Questions to ask your teenager:

▶ Have you been certain of a particular career path throughout high school?
▶ Do you tell everyone you have "no idea" of your future after college?

Questions to ask regarding college choices:

▶ Is the institution primarily a liberal arts college, or does it primarily train pre-professional students?
▶ Is there a way to focus seriously on one major but explore other academic areas as well?

Family discussion questions:

▶ What were your favorite activities over the past few years?
▶ If you could have any job in the world, what would it be?
▶ What is the most important part of going to college?

CONSERVATIVE<————————————————————>LIBERAL

We all have different comfort zones involving social, cultural, and religious values. Knowing what will allow your teenager to feel at ease, or make him uncomfortable, are critical assessments. One aspect of this feeling of comfort is how we view ourselves on the continuum of conservative versus liberal—including social, cultural, and political issues.

George comes from a close-knit religious family whose values are culturally conservative. He's uncomfortable with what he perceives to be non-traditional behavior (such as men and women living together before marriage), and he's most comfortable being with people like himself. His comfort zone is clearly delineated. George attends the oldest independent school in his state, and he believes he wants to continue his higher education in an environment that will parallel his high school experience.

Bill, on the other hand, attends a large inner-city high school. The population of his school is diverse, and Bill enjoys the cultural exchange that goes on in his school's environment. He too wishes to find a college that will parallel his high school. But he wants to attend a college that devotes considerable resources to political and social activism.

Bill and George are on the extreme ends of this spectrum; however, most teenagers as well as adults will see themselves as falling somewhere between these two end points. One may be conservative in some areas, such as clothing, but liberal in other areas, such as supporting immigrant rights. One can be liberal in some areas, like advocating for medical use of marijuana, but generally conservative in regard to other issues.

> ∾One aspect of this feeling of comfort is how we view ourselves on the continuum of conservative versus liberal—including social, cultural, and political issues.∾

Discussing these issues can improve family communication and rapport. How do you feel about various social and political issues? Where would you place yourself on this continuum? Where would you place your son or daughter? Do you and your teenager arrive at the same conclusions about one another?

Understanding each person's values can help direct the college search. Is your student going to be more comfortable in a single-sex or coeducational setting? Is your daughter comfortable with a diversity of viewpoints, or is her comfort zone more circumscribed? Would a large public university meet your teenager's need for diversity better than a small liberal arts college? These are questions to consider both when first exploring possible college options, and then again when actually visiting various institutions.

Questions to ask your teenager:

▶ How would you have voted in the last presidential election?
▶ How do feel when you have to defend an unpopular viewpoint to your peers?

Questions to ask regarding college choices:

▶ Do you feel comfortable surrounded by people with different viewpoints?
▶ If so, would you be comfortable if two-thirds of those around you held views that differed from your own?

Family discussion questions:

▶ In general, do you think this is a good time to be growing up?
▶ How do you think your generation and your parents' generation are different or the same?

INTELLECTUALLY FOCUSED<————>SOCIALLY FOCUSED

Not all high school students are—or should be—college bound. During each of the past twenty years, 60 to 65 percent of graduating American high school seniors moved on immediately to some form of higher education. A large percentage of this group, almost two million students per year, goes on to college because they don't know what else to do. Many consider college to be a rite of passage to the next stage of development and maturity. Depending on a student's personality, that passage is viewed primarily through a social lens or a cognitive, intellectual lens.

Linda has loved to read books for as long as she can remember. She has always associated school with comfort and success. She enjoys learning new skills and ideas. Linda has actively sought out new intellectual avenues of growth, including various courses at the local community college, while taking as many Advanced Placement courses as she could. Linda has seen high school as a means to get to college, where the intellectual stimulation will be greater and even more rewarding. Linda knows that, for her, college is all about the pursuit of knowledge. Given her personality, it's imperative for her to find a college that nourishes the minds of the students as much as possible. Social development takes a back seat to learning, as far as Linda is concerned.

Justin is extremely bright, and he's always been an outstanding student. He has terrific grades and SAT scores. However, he prefers video games to novels, and he enjoys socializing with his friends more than cracking the books. Justin would argue that he learns the most important life skills from his social interactions. He loves to share ideas, but his thoughts are not all about intellectual pursuits. Justin is impassioned on the subject of sports—you name one, he loves it. His other passion is computers. He has no expectations, though, that he'll pursue either of these interests while in college.

He's eager to go to college so he can meet new people with whom he can socialize. He considers college another step on the road to reaching adulthood. But he's happy that he will have four more years to be an adolescent before he has to surrender to the proverbial 9-to-5 workday. Justin knows he wants to join a fraternity, and he'll be very concerned about the quality of the night scene on his college campus. He's also interested in attending a school where the student body is fanatical about its sports teams.

Both Justin and Linda could be strong candidates for many colleges and universities. They're both bright and perform well on various measures of adolescent achievement. However, given their very different personality styles and interests, they will look for different things from a college. A top-tier school for one may be the wrong choice for the other.

Where do you feel your teenager belongs on the intellectual-social continuum?

Questions to ask your teenager:

- What do you read for fun?
- Which do you enjoy more, socializing or reading?

Questions to ask regarding college choices:

▶   What percentage of your time do you expect to be studying?
▶   What percentage of your time do you expect to be socializing?
▶   How important are discussion-based classes to you?
▶   Do you want to be in an environment in which students tend to discuss ideas late into the night?

Family discussion questions:

▶   What do you like to do most on Saturday night?
▶   What do you like to do most on a rainy Sunday?
▶   What do you usually spend most of your time doing on weekends?

LINEAR<————————————————————————>NON-LINEAR

Some of us think inductively (reasoning from the particular to the general) while others think deductively (from the general to the particular). In terms of temperament, some of us think in linear terms, while others are more global in our reactions and responses to the environment around us. Another way to explore this dimension is to consider the notion of traditional versus nontraditional thinkers.

Do you try to solve problems by thinking inside or outside the box? Where do you and your teenager fall on this spectrum? Does she tend to think in terms of traditional resolutions to problems, such as, "How do I earn more money for a car?" Does your child gravitate to traditional adolescent jobs (cashier, waiter, salesclerk, etc.), or is she more likely to explore nontraditional options, such as starting her own business? Does your teenager see career paths predetermined by traditional models (doctor, lawyer, accountant, etc.), or is she interested in creating a novel enterprise? Early entrepreneurs often indicate a desire to be creative or non-linear in their approach to problem solving. Those of us who tend to be more artistic also tend to think and behave in a less-traditional, non-linear manner.

Chris is an exceptionally talented musician. He plays the guitar whenever he has the opportunity, and his passion is music of any kind. He has been sure of a career in the music world since he was in junior high school. However, he's not sure, despite his talent, that he can make it as a professional guitarist.

Chris sees solutions to problems differently from many of his friends. He knows he needs experience as well as connections in the music world to further his career ambitions. He has used his creativity to try to get some recognition for his talent. Instead of directly applying for musician jobs or trying to start his own band, he's considering applying for jobs that would allow him to meet professional musicians—including jobs at recording studios and concert venues. He's an excellent student academically, but he's struggling with the decision to attend college. Should he go to a music program? A university where he can major in music? Should he go to college at all, or just jump into the field as some sort of music apprentice?

Ruth's father is a doctor, and her mother is a lawyer. She's always assumed that she would attend college as a stepping-stone to a professional career. She has planned her four years in high school with the goal of loading up on Advanced Placement courses and developing strong college applications. Ruth's thinking is quite linear and traditional. Step One: Take challenging courses, get good grades, study for the SATs, and develop a strong resume that will look good on her college applications. Step Two: Apply to the most competitive schools she can possibly get into; given the choice, go to the highest-ranked college to which she is accepted. Step Three: Work hard in college to obtain the highest GPA she can in order to have the best chance of admission to the graduate programs of her choice.

Ruth and Chris will more than likely be successful adults. They're both motivated and feel driven toward goals. Ruth's path is more traditional and linear. She instinctively moves from A to B to C. Chris, on the other hand, knows roughly where he wants to end up, but he's not sure how to get there. His personality is well suited to this uncertainty. He's comfortable with taking a non-linear approach to his growth and development. He sees many options available to him, and he feels comfortable exploring and experimenting. For him, life is more like the spokes on a wheel than a straight trail to his destination. Chris may go down some dead-end paths, but he's confident that he'll eventually get where he wants to be.

How do you feel about this way of looking at the world? How do you problem solve? Do you and your spouse tend to be more linear in how you approach a dilemma? Is your child similar to you or different? The way you and your teenager approach the college selection process itself may give you clues. When looking at specific colleges, you may want to investigate how most classes are conducted: are they mostly lectures, or is there a focus on learning while doing? Are small classes aimed at creative problem solving or are the courses taught in a lecture/exam mode?

Questions to ask your teenager:

- Do you like to solve problems creatively?
- Do you gravitate toward traditional adolescent job opportunities?

Questions to ask regarding college choices:

- What are classes like at various colleges? Are they mostly small-group discussions or large lectures?
- Is there an emphasis on independent study?

Family discussion questions:

- What is your favorite game?
- What subject do you enjoy studying or reading about the most?
- If you were dropped in a foreign land and did not speak the language, how would you find where you were and how to get home?

SELF-MOTIVATED<————————————>EXTERNALLY MOTIVATED

Many parents say they're unable to get their teenager to do anything—make the bed, go to school on time, do homework . . . the list can go on and on. Your child's personality may have always been either internally driven or externally driven. Recall his or her earlier childhood: Did your daughter want to learn a sport, or did you have to entice her? Did your son do his homework on his own, or did you have to nag him endlessly? Did your daughter call up to make an appointment for her driver's test, or did you have to do it for her? Is your teenager still relying on you (and others) to motivate him, or is he self-motivated?

Each child comes into the world with a personality predisposition. One child decides on her own to learn how to ride a bicycle and keeps at it, no matter how many times she falls off. On the other hand, the externally driven child is often eager to please adults and looks to them for cues about her behavior.

Mike's parents call him a real self-starter. They feel extremely fortunate that they never have to nag him about his chores or getting his schoolwork finished. Mike sets his own alarm clock, gets himself off to school on his own, and takes pride in his own accomplishments. While he's popular at school, he has little interest in holding any positions of authority in any of his activities. He plays on the high school football team, yet he has turned down offers to become team captain. Mike seems to like to do things on his own, with little concern about how others respond to him. While he's extremely likable and successful, he's more interested in paying attention to his own goals rather than those others set for him.

Knowing your child's personality predisposition will be tremendously helpful in the admissions process. You can anticipate where you may need to step in and where you may have to step back.

Emma has a passion for soccer, but there always seems to be a struggle to get her to practice. She takes her greatest pleasure in knowing her friends and family are proud of her achievements. She wants one of her parents to be at all her soccer games. Emma thrives on positive reinforcement from those around her. She is motivated to excel by the knowledge that she will make those who care about her happy. Her parents recognize that they will have to be an active part of Emma's college search and that she would thrive in a college that emphasizes group learning.

Take this opportunity to recall your own personality as a teenager. How did you handle external pressures? Did you rely on others to motivate you? Or were you adamant about accomplishing things on your own? How did you and your parents resolve disagreements?

Knowing your child's personality predisposition will be tremendously helpful in the admissions process. You can anticipate where you may need to step in and where you may have to step back. How will your child go about making a college selection? Will she insist on doing everything herself? Or will she rely on you and your spouse to do all the heavy lifting? This awareness should reduce the number and severity of potential conflicts that can arise during this emotionally charged period.

Questions to ask your teenager:

▶   Do you enjoy planning your own extracurricular activities?
▶   Do you do your homework without being prompted?

Questions to ask regarding college choices:

▶   Do you tend to do better work in groups or by yourself?
▶   Do you think you'll need regular check-ins with professors or advisors?

Family discussion questions:

▶   If you didn't need to have a job, what would you do with your time?
▶   If you were a multimillionaire, how would you use your money?
▶   If you knew you wouldn't receive a speeding ticket when you were driving, what would you do?

11

Key Aspects of College Applications

If you and your family know how the admissions process unfolds, including what needs to happen and when, then you'll be able to talk about what tasks have to be done and by whom.

While we can't provide a personal strategic guide for every reader, we have outlined, for your reference, the major aspects of college applications.

BENEFITING FROM CAMPUS VISITS

Visits to college campuses will enable your child to physically visualize life after high school and to see that there are a variety of educational options open to him. It also will help you imagine where and how your child may fit into different college environments.

Many families combine college visits with other interests. Ideally, you'll be able to focus on shared interests that your entire family enjoys, including those of younger siblings. Are you interested in baseball parks or historic inns? You could visit two colleges, take in a baseball game, and stay at a bed and breakfast all in one long weekend.

In terms of the campus visit itself, we suggest that you wear comfortable shoes—and a smile. The real purpose of a campus visit is to get a sense of whether or not your child feels comfortable at that particular college. An official campus tour and admissions office information session can be helpful at the beginning stages of your search, but you need to get out there on

141

campus and interact with those who aren't being paid to tell you good things about the school.

This is where your son or daughter's smile comes in. Go to the main campus dining hall. Grab something to drink, smile, and talk with random students. You and your college-bound teenager can start up conversations about their experiences. "Do you like it here?" "Where do you come from?" "Why did you choose to come here in the first place?" "In what ways is this college satisfying and not satisfying your expectations?" The answers to these questions will help your child determine whether he'll want to spend four years on that campus.

It's remarkable how much information you can glean from these discussions. They may raise red flags for you or your student. Conversely, current college students may point out aspects of the college that could be extremely appealing to you and your teenager. Can you imagine your child fitting in with this student body? Does your student feel it is a comfortable fit? The emotional connection to a place—positive, negative, or neutral—is not usually evident until you actually set foot on a campus and mingle with the student body.

> ∽An official campus tour and admissions office information session can be helpful at the beginning stages of your search, but you need to get out there on campus and interact with those who aren't being paid to tell you good things about the school.∽

WHEN TO APPLY FOR ADMISSION

Deadlines are extremely important in the college admissions world. Generally, high school seniors submit their college applications during the fall immediately preceding the year in which they hope to enroll. As of the writing of this book, there are five major plans through which your child can apply.

Regular decision involves submitting an application to a college, often by January 1st, and then waiting approximately three months for an answer. If accepted, then your child usually has one month to decide whether or not to attend.

Early decision. In an attempt to increase enrollment or to make the college appear more selective than it would be through the free market of regular decision, a college may offer its applicants the option of applying under an early decision plan. Early decision usually involves a commitment on the part of the university to review an application within six to eight weeks, with the understanding that students are generally committed to attending that university if accepted. Early decision helps universities appear more desirable because the schools can later boast that almost 100 percent of a significant segment of their incoming class chose to attend that institution over any other.

Under most early decision programs, prospective students apply by November 1st, and colleges notify them by December 15th as to whether they've been accepted, rejected, or deferred. If your student is accepted, then he is by and large bound to attend that college. If he is denied admission, then he may not attend that college. If he is deferred, it will be noted on his file that he applied early decision, and in a few months he will be re-evaluated in the context of the regular decision applicants.

Early decision II generally carries with it the same terms and conditions as early decision, but with a later deadline. Most early decision II applications are due in January, and colleges usually commit to responding by some time in February.

Early action usually follows the same timeline as early decision with one key difference: students are not required to commit to attending a college that accepts them under an early action plan. Students may wait until they hear from other schools applied to under regular decision, and choose from among their choices by May 1st.

Rolling decision is a plan by which universities evaluate applications on a first-come, first-served basis. Rather than waiting to evaluate applications during a regular decision round, the admissions committees at many of the larger universities meet every few weeks and admit a number of students from the current pool of applicants. Under rolling admissions, students who apply earlier usually receive their admissions decisions earlier—without a commitment to attend that university. Students can usually send in rolling decision applications beginning some time in the fall.

It's almost always to a student's advantage to apply earlier rather than later. While some students need their senior year grades to demonstrate an upward academic trend, this consideration is often offset by there being a greater number of freshman seats available earlier in the admissions cycle.

Not all universities offer all admissions plans, and universities are notorious for changing their admissions plans and deadlines frequently in order to try to outmaneuver competitor institutions.

Regardless of which admissions plans most interest your child, we recommend that you urge your teenager to take advantage of rolling decision options where available. Admissions committee responses to rolling decision applications can help him judge whether his other college choices are practical. If he receives an early acceptance, he can pare down his list of other schools, or if not admitted, he can expand his college list.

WHAT IS INCLUDED IN THE APPLICATION?

Transcripts

The most important piece of a college application is undoubtedly the high school transcript. Make sure that your child's transcript is correct and up-to-date. Don't wait until applications need to be sent out to colleges to review the transcript. Make sure it accurately reflects all the courses taken, honors or AP designations, and correct grades received.

Standardized Tests

You should make sure that your child registers to take her standardized tests. The two most popular are the SAT and the ACT. Increasingly, students are taking both in the hopes that they might fare better on one or the other. There are numerous books and study guides on how to prepare for both tests. We urge your child to pick up one of these books, preferably one that includes test-taking strategies. Better yet, seriously prepare for whichever test your student prefers by taking a review course or hiring a tutor.

~It's almost always to a student's advantage to apply earlier rather than later.~

Letters of Recommendation

One or two letters of recommendation may be required as part of your child's applications. Generally, these letters should be from teachers who have taught your student in a classroom setting. Be sure to encourage your child to ask her teachers well in advance for these letters. They take time to prepare carefully; therefore, many teachers limit the number of students for whom they will write.

Ideally, your student will ask her teacher for the recommendation toward the end of the academic year, when your daughter's performance is fresh in the teacher's mind. Most colleges accept letters from ninth and tenth grade teachers, but it's preferable, if possible, to have letters from teachers who have taught your child in her junior year.

High school guidance counselors usually include a school letter of recommendation along with your child's transcript. It's incumbent upon your child to make sure she gets to know her counselor personally so that the counselor can write a personalized letter. You as a parent should consult regularly with your child's high school guidance counselor. Good admissions counselors can help you understand how the subtleties of the application process are likely to affect your child. Moreover, counselors can help your child on a case-by-case basis with essays and school selection.

Essays

Some parents are tempted to take on the challenge of writing essays for their student's college applications. We urge you to encourage and support your child's efforts, but do not write her essays for her. We know that a great many students every year drag their feet on this part of the application process, hoping their parents will just break down and write the essays for them. Don't do it!

Even the most junior college admissions officer can tell when a parent has written an applicant's essay. And besides, do you really want to hold your child's hand through every step of the process? Do yourself a favor: let your child's high school guidance counselor or educational consultant fill that role. Experienced counselors know how much essay help they should and should not give.

We cannot emphasize enough the importance of multiple essay drafts. Even the best writers in the world find that they can improve upon their first drafts after allowing some time for reflection. Encourage your child to write a draft—and then to do nothing more on it for a week or so. When she looks at her essay after the week has gone by, she'll likely find some things that she wants to add, delete, or change. If she repeats this process, her essay almost certainly will improve.

Often students get frustrated when they begin working on their essays. If beautiful prose doesn't just come out in ten minutes, they give up and come up with lots of other things they need to do. Help your child to not be afraid of trying to put her initial thoughts on paper—even if they are just random thoughts. All writers

~Even the most junior college admissions officer can tell when a parent has written an applicant's essay.~

need to start somewhere. Bring in her favorite Chinese food, light candles, or put on some Mozart. Whatever you do, encourage her to put something down on paper before she gets frustrated and decides to quit for the day.

Once your student has gotten past this initial bout with writer's block, help her think objectively about what she has written. What sort of impression would an admissions reader have about her from that particular essay? Ask your teenager if she is happy about leaving that impression.

This is usually a good starting point for some discussion about the essay. Do what you can to gently explain to your child that just because she has had a certain experience doesn't mean that thousands of others haven't had somewhat similar ones. "How My Varsity Sport Has Taught Me Leadership Skills" is one of the most common—and boring—college essays written by thousands of students every year.

PREPARING TO APPLY FOR FINANCIAL AID

While your child is working on her essays, we suggest that you assemble the materials necessary to apply for financial aid. Your last three years of federal and state tax returns, bank account statements, and records of real estate transactions will usually be enough to get you started.

Many families hire an accountant or certified financial planner to assist with various forms. If you decide to approach financial aid on your own, remember that the financial aid officer is not your friend. Just as insurance adjusters always seem to evaluate claims to the advantage of the insurance company, so too do college financial aid officers usually err on the side of interpretations that benefit the college—and award you fewer aid dollars.

We strongly advise you to seek professional assistance with financial aid forms. The financial stakes to you and your family are just too high to make a mistake or to allow a college to provide you with an unreasonably low financial aid package.

DECIDING WHERE TO APPLY

There can be a great deal of tension surrounding where your child ultimately wants to apply to college. Sometimes, the whole family agrees with all the choices. Often, though, there are sharp differences in the views of various family members. In a common admissions scenario, the mother is focused on distance from home, the father is focused on cost and the economic value of a particular college's degree, and the teenager just wants to find a school where he can meet new friends.

~Often students get frustrated when they begin working on their essays. If beautiful prose doesn't just come out in ten minutes, they give up and come up with lots of other things they need to do.~

A good strategy is to create a checklist that includes the major factors that are relevant to your family. Each family member should make his or her own list. Rate the factors on a scale of 1 to 10, with 1 being unimportant and 10 being the most important. This list could include, but not necessarily be limited to, medical needs, learning support, geographic location, course offerings, school size, extracurricular activities, and internship opportunities.

A visual representation can help you see more clearly where all members of your family agree. Begin drawing up the college list using the areas of agreement as a guide. If there are significant differences of opinion, have a family discussion about the need to reach agreement about the unresolved factors. There may need to be some compromise. Perhaps you believe that your child needs learning support services at college, but he feels he does not. Select schools then that interest your child and, at the same time, have the resources you believe he needs.

TIME MANAGEMENT ISSUES

Expecting your child to carefully complete all his college applications well in advance of the deadlines and without some parental prodding is normally unrealistic.

Again, we suggest that you set aside a particular time, preferably an hour or so on the same day each week, to speak with your child about his application progress. Think about this as being a little like office hours with a professor. Your student will know that he will be asked about his progress, which in itself is helpful for him. This schedule means that family members won't have to argue with him a few times a week about his college applications.

During the spring before senior year, encourage your child to obtain last year's application from each college to which he plans to apply. Have your child find the target date for the release of the application forms for his application year. Begin to scope out what information will likely be required: what the essays tend to look like, recommendation letters or standardized tests that are usually needed, and probable deadlines. Once your child has the current application, you can help him plan for how long it might take to complete it—including writing the essays and assembling other required materials.

Your student still will need to do his applications, of course. But mapping out timelines and tasks can help everyone in the family feel more in control of the process. If you provide your child with a little breathing room —within a structure—you can make the application process move along more smoothly.

12

The Long Wait for Decisions

For many students and families, the relief of having all the applications sent out, usually by January 1st, can be a liberating experience. Parents and teenagers will have been consumed, often for many years, with concerns about preparing for the college admissions process. Completing this process can, and should be, a cause for celebration. At last, your student can begin to enjoy her senior year. You can all sit back, take a deep breath, and begin to get some perspective—until the decisions come in around April 1st.

Many parents report that during the second semester of their teen's senior year, they were emotionally closer to their adolescent than they had been in years. Most family members realize that an end to one era of family life is fast approaching. You can now slow down and enjoy being together. The demands of many high schools tend to diminish during the second half of senior year, and, often for the first time in years, your student may have extra time on her hands. Use this time to do things together. Plan more family outings and stay involved with one another.

Try to put the whole college choice question on hold for a few months. Think about it like going on vacation. You know your work will still be there when you get back, but enjoy your time off while you can.

DEALING WITH THOSE WHO HAVE ALREADY BEEN ACCEPTED
Friends and neighbors may have children who have already been accepted early decision and know where they are going in the fall. Others may have

heard from colleges with rolling admissions, so they know some of their options while still waiting until April to hear about others. They'll have a certain level of relief, knowing that they have been accepted somewhere.

Most applicants to U.S. universities do not apply under early decision programs. Thus, there are thousands of other high school seniors who are waiting until April just like your son or daughter. Don't let the cacophony of other families' discussions about their child's acceptance drown out your rational voice. Just because your child has not gotten into a school yet does not mean that she will not get in at the appointed time.

Avoid discussions about college with friends, neighbors, and others who all of a sudden seem to have a vested interest in your student's future. Tell people who want to talk about colleges that you don't want to enter into these discussions before April 1st. For now, you and your family are taking a leave of absence from all the college application pressure.

> ∾Don't let the cacophony of other families' discussions about their child's acceptance drown out your rational voice.∾

This is the time to refocus and enjoy the moment. Your child's second semester of senior year will be filled with memorable moments. When will she play her last high school varsity game? When will she have her last art exhibit? When will she complete work on the senior yearbook? When will she take her last Advanced Placement exam?

High schools have their own, sometimes unique, events to mark the close of the year for each senior class. There are usually numerous activities to celebrate the achievements of twelfth graders: senior banquets, sporting events, award ceremonies, and the prom. While many of these events will not take place until April or May, often weeks of preparation lead up to them. Encourage your student to participate in as many of these activities as possible. This may also be your last chance to volunteer at your teenager's school. Use this time to craft your own leave-taking from teachers and fellow parents.

Make sure you record your student's final year in high school. Take photos and videos whenever possible. Also use this time to look back on your adolescent's childhood. This is a wonderful opportunity to bring out baby books and old photos.

HOW TO HANDLE TENSION

No matter how hard you try to take a break from the college admissions process, it may seem to follow you everywhere. Don't be surprised if each family member experiences some tension about the long wait for decisions, especially if your student applied early decision or early action and was not admitted. Receiving any letters of rejection, or even a deferral, may make you feel more anxious during the wait. It may feel difficult to stay in a positive frame of mind.

Do your best to remain upbeat. One rejection does not add up to total rejection. Often the early decision school is one that is fiercely competitive for even the most accomplished students. Therefore, try not to allow this early rejection to become an emotional devastation.

The more your family is involved in positive activities, the less influence others can have on your emotions. Give some thought to what each family member finds most relaxing and make sure you take the time to do at least some of these activities.

Here are some ideas for reducing stress:

- Exercise—which can include taking regular walks.
- Take a warm shower or a bubble bath.
- Treat yourself to something you enjoy—it can even be a special food treat, like an ice cream cone.
- Go to lots of movies.
- Read a good book.
- Call up (not e-mail) a friend you haven't spoken to in a while.
- Go out of town for a quick getaway.
- Stay in town and do something you haven't done in a long time—go to a museum or a nearby park.
- Get a massage.
- Listen to some soothing music, especially before going to sleep.

READING BETWEEN THE LINES: YOUR TEEN AND STRESS

Some teenagers pretend that everything is okay, even though they're worried to death. It is difficult for students to disengage emotionally from the college search, particularly if many of their peers have already decided what college they'll be attending, or if school conversation continues to focus obsessively on the admissions process. While your student may be acting as if she is unconcerned, you need to sense if there are some worries bubbling below the surface.

Take a proactive stance. Try to get your teenager to talk about her feelings of uncertainty. Acknowledge that her feelings are understandable. Don't tell her how she should feel. Listen and reflect on what you hear. Is she envious of some of her friends? Is she worried that she'll be rejected by all her colleges? Is she anxious about leaving high school and moving on? Is she questioning her previous decisions? You may even hear, "I know I applied to all the wrong schools. None of them will be right for me!"

At this point, your child's emotions may be entangled with yours. It may be difficult for you to distinguish what is driving which feelings. But don't panic. This is a totally predictable reaction to the process.

Students are usually able to keep their college search in some perspective. However, make sure your child is not showing any signs of depression. While being depressed may not necessarily be tied directly to the college admissions process, this is a period in which emotional stress may trigger an underlying difficulty. If you're not sure how distressed your child is feeling, ask her.

~Students are usually able to keep their college search in some perspective. However, make sure your child is not showing any signs of depression.~

Many teenagers will not initiate a conversation about how they are feeling, but if you inquire and show your concern, they usually will answer relatively directly. Demonstrate that you care and that you're there to be supportive in a nonjudgmental manner. If you're concerned about the depth of your child's anxiety or depression, make sure you contact your doctor about a mental health referral. It's always better to err on the side of caution.

Having the opportunity to sort out her emotions with a therapist may be extremely helpful. You want to ensure your child's well-being, and you also want to make sure that choices made in April will be based on rational decision making. Furthermore, you want to make sure your child will be in the best position to adapt to college in the fall.

Discourage your anxious teen from worrying about what might happen. Explain to her that there are so many permutations and combinations of which universities she will or will not get into (with or without different aid packages), that obsessively focusing on what might or might not occur when decision e-mails and letters arrive will only increase everyone's level of anxiety.

~If you're focused on your own bruised ego, then you'll be less available to help your child emotionally move past rejection and into the positive aspects of making a choice. When people feel in control, they almost always feel better about their position.~

UNCERTAINTY ABOUT OFFERS AND FINANCIAL AID PACKAGES

As April approaches, it's likely that you and your family will face increasing uncertainty about pending admissions and financial aid decisions. Who wouldn't be nervous about getting a "yes" or "no" from an admissions committee—along with the wide range of possible $0-$200,000 financial aid packages?

In just a few weeks, your teenager will know the results of her efforts. We hope that your child will be admitted to the schools of her choice and receive generous aid packages. However, we all know that it's unlikely that all the schools of your dreams will admit your child, let alone give her a full scholarship.

If your teenager is the rare student who is admitted everywhere with a full merit award, then you should skip ahead to the next chapter. Most students will need to choose from offers that include some financial aid and other offers of admission only. From these choices, your child will need to determine which college best meets her criteria for happiness. Is it the school that's closest to home? Farthest away? Most prestigious? The one with the best political science department?

Before any rational decision making can occur, though, your teenager must be given the time and space to "grieve" for lost opportunities—the schools from which she was rejected. This is extremely important because it can be difficult to focus on making a selection from other schools if your child's heart was set on something different.

Try to get your teenager to look at the positive aspects of the school choices that are available to her. Understand, however, that you're working against the psychological pull that what we can't have often looks more appealing than what we can have.

You can play a vital role in helping your student not experience rejection as a personal insult. But this is easier said than done—especially if you've gotten caught up in the process by placing your own ego on the line. Not only is it possible for you to ache over your child's rejection, but you may also feel rejected as well.

Rejection may spark old issues about past rebuffs either received by you or your child. Old emotional wounds can be reopened, which can lead to depression, anxiety, or irritability. You may vividly relive your own feelings about the end of your high school years. Did you go to college? Were you rejected from your first-choice college? Did other circumstances keep you from going to a particular college?

If you're focused on your own bruised ego, then you'll be less available to help your child emotionally move past rejection and into the positive aspects of making a choice. When people feel in control, they almost always feel better about their position. Encourage your teenager to recognize where she can make decisions and assert control. Help your child recognize the truth of what we've said before: there isn't one perfect school for each student. Your child can be happy and successful at many places.

At the end of April, uncertainty usually turns to acceptance as most students come to realize that they have to choose from the schools and financial aid packages on the table. The waiting is over. Now you and your student must make some important decisions.

13

Making a Wise Choice

It's decision time. After the months and years of hard work, worrying, and difficult family discussions, you must now choose from the college options available to your child.

As simple as it may seem, it's a good idea to make a list of the colleges that have accepted your son or daughter. Then, as a family, begin to discuss the pros and cons of each institution. At this point, don't discard any schools from the list.

Next, you, your spouse, and your teenager should list different facets of life at each college that you believe will be important over the next four years. Some topics to include are the size of school, distance from home, strength of academic departments, cost, financial aid packages, housing options, fraternity or sorority life, sports programs, extracurricular activities on and around campus, internship possibilities, study abroad opportunities, and male-female ratios. Perhaps most important, can your child see himself as an integral part of the student body?

Pretend that the admissions process never happened. By doing so, you can begin looking at your student's current options in a fresh way. If your child applied to ten schools, for instance, and was admitted to four of them, then look at these four institutions only.

Be supportive of your child's accomplishments, regardless of how many schools accepted him. Encourage your child to feel good about all of his options by reminding him that, unlike the admissions stage of the process, he is now in control.

Think about this like going out to eat. Before leaving, you may have your mind set on eating pancakes. However, when you get to the restaurant, you discover that breakfast is no longer being served. You can become upset and even threaten to go home. But if you're hungry, there's sure to be something else on the menu that may be satisfying in the end, especially if you acknowledge you still have some choices.

Recognizing when you do have choices and that you can make decisions can be an emotionally invigorating experience. Encourage your student to take pride and pleasure in the choices he now has. Now you all can take a deep breath and get ready to re-evaluate which school will be the best fit.

> Recognizing when you do have choices and that you can make decisions can be an emotionally invigorating experience.

You and your child may want to revisit, or visit for the first time, the schools that accepted him. It's likely that acceptance will color his views. This is a good thing: it's easier to objectively look at a school once you know that it's truly possible to attend.

A faculty member or student from a college to which your child was accepted may call to see if your teenager has any questions. It may feel flattering to be wooed in this manner, especially if the contact comes on the heels of a number of rejection letters in April. Remember, though, at this point, the focus should be on whether the college satisfies your child's needs—not the other way around.

Just as various members of your family probably had different views during the admissions process, you all may very well have different ideas about the pros and cons of the colleges that sent acceptance letters. Everyone's views may have changed during the admissions process. So, even if you think you know the views of your spouse or child, it's worth re-checking how everyone now perceives the college choices. You're likely to be surprised by how your own views may have changed throughout the process as well.

COMPARING COLLEGE CHOICES

A good place to start is the academic department that most interests your teenager. How good is it? What interesting courses have been offered in the last few years? Has the department been able to help undergraduates get internships in the field? Are the current students pleased with the way professors teach and interact with them? Are classes usually taught as discussion seminars or lectures? Do professors primarily teach the undergraduate courses, or do graduate students do the bulk of the work?

Assessing the overall quality and prestige of various institutions can be difficult. Some family members may focus on the *U.S. News & World Report* college rankings, while others may base their feelings about particular schools on personal experiences. Teenagers tend to judge colleges based on their own set of factors. Did someone whom they respect from their high school choose to attend or not attend a particular college? Parents often draw on how they perceived certain schools when they were applying to colleges. Talk to other students from your hometown, parents whose children are currently enrolled, and expert third parties who can help you evaluate the current merits of each school.

If money is a factor, carefully examine how much it will cost for your child to attend each college or university. We recommend making a yearly budget for each school, factoring in tuition, fees, books, and travel, as well as the grants and loans that are part of your child's financial aid package. Because financial aid packages are generally good for one year, it makes sense to compare one year of education costs at one school with one year of education costs at the other institutions.

You might be surprised to find that in some cases the school with the highest tuition will actually cost you the least amount of money. This can happen if your child's financial aid package includes a large grant or scholarship. Additionally, when you start researching travel options, you might discover that a particular plane, bus, or train route is not as expensive as you had previously thought.

> You might be surprised to find that in some cases the school with the highest tuition will actually cost you the least amount of money.

After having done your research about the colleges that accepted your teenager, you and your family should again discuss the pros and cons of each school. Hopefully, the time spent researching academic departments, relative overall quality, and cost will lead to a decision that pleases everyone. If not, you'll need to discuss who will be empowered to make the final decision.

We believe that students ultimately should have the final word as to where they would like to go to school. After all, it's your son or daughter who will actually be attending college. If he has chosen the most expensive option on the table, however, then you as a parent certainly have the right to insist that he be willing to contribute financially toward his preferred college.

Some parents refuse to pay for any of their child's education unless their son or daughter chooses the college that most pleases one or both parents. This stance may be rather punitive, and you need to be aware that it can cause a serious rift in your relationship with your child. Unless the issue is strictly about finances, remind yourself that your child is the one who needs to be happy and successful at his chosen school. Fortunately, if there has been sufficient exploration and discussion over the previous months about college options, this scenario is unlikely to unfold.

Hopefully, if you have strong reasons for not wanting your child to attend a certain institution, you made this known well before the April acceptance letters arrived. However, if you believe that your child is truly making a grave mistake, you need to try to convince him of the wisdom of your views. You may want to invite other family members or friends to talk with him as well.

ONE FAMILY'S DECISION DILEMMA

While Samantha was rising to become editor-in-chief of her high school newspaper, she dreamed about attending Syracuse University because of its highly regarded communications program. She carefully researched various colleges, and when she became a high school senior she informed her parents that Syracuse University, although private and expensive, was her first choice.

To maintain the peace in her family regarding cost, Samantha decided to apply to Syracuse regular decision, along with a wide range of other expensive and not-so-expensive regular decision colleges. Her father was uncomfortable with the price tags of the expensive schools, but went along with the list of colleges because he recognized that there was no real harm in just applying.

In April, Samantha was admitted to a number of schools, including Syracuse, which offered her a few thousand dollars of financial aid. Even with this package, though, Syracuse would still cost more than some of the other colleges that had admitted Samantha. Her father's position about cost hadn't changed. Meanwhile, Samantha was ecstatic that she'd been admitted to her first-choice college.

Samantha's father told her that while he supported her journalistic interests, he could not justify to himself the incredibly high tuition charges at Syracuse. Surely, some of the other colleges, with similar communications programs but with dissimilar price tags, would also provide a good quality education and help Samantha's future career. But Samantha had done her research and carefully explained to her father the tangible benefits that she would get by attending Syracuse.

Her father still could not understand why he should pay many thousands of dollars a year more for what his daughter could more or less get at a lower-priced institution. Samantha's mother refused to take sides but suggested that Samantha and her dad talk with Samantha's college advisor to help break the deadlock.

After some intense discussion, it became clear that there was a real deadlock. The data provided by Samantha about the educational quality and career benefits of a Syracuse education still could not convince her father to pay for Samantha's choice. Through the discussion, Samantha came to understand that the tuition charges at Syracuse would cause financial hardships for her family.

Samantha's family was able to reach a compromise that worked for them. Her father agreed to pay for what it would have cost her to attend the college he believed would offer her a good education at an acceptable tuition, and then offered to help her take out the necessary loans to finance the difference.

As a general rule, we don't think it's unreasonable to ask students to take out manageable student loans. An education is an investment—and in most cases, investments require people to put money at risk. Many parents ultimately come to realize that the final decision, even if it's an expensive one, ought to be made by their student. Parents then try to "find" some money to lessen the amount of their child's student loan.

WAIT LISTS

Colleges use wait lists as a sort of insurance policy. They want to make sure that they completely fill the number of available freshman seats.

The number of students admitted off wait lists can be extremely small. In two recent years, both Harvard and Ohio State admitted no one from their wait lists. Out of thousands of applicants, Emory University accepted only twenty-five students off the wait list during the same period. Georgetown University took ten people off its wait list—out of 15,000 applicants. And in one recent year, Columbia University placed more students on the wait list than they accepted overall.

The positive by-product of placing increasingly large numbers of students on the wait list is that colleges soften the blow to more students who ultimately are not admitted, especially children of alumni. Families can now say they were on the Columbia wait list, rather than knowing that their children were rejected.

Given the low odds of your child, or any child, being accepted off a selective college wait list, we advise you to make your family decision about school choice from the options available in April. May 1st is the common reply date by which you will need to choose one of these options. Since most colleges can't even look thoroughly at their wait lists until after that date, you and your family should proceed as if there really was no wait list.

Make your decision from the schools and financial aid offers on the table. If at a later date, your child is admitted off a wait list, you can then take the same family approach to evaluating options that you did before. This time, of course, there would be only two options from which to choose: the school your child selected by May 1st and the school that had previously put your son or daughter on its wait list.

A college can inform your child that he has been accepted as late as the day before classes begin. It's not impossible, therefore, for your child to have put down a deposit, arranged student housing, and paid a semester's tuition to one school, when all of a sudden you're faced with a changed landscape.

You and your child might have only a few days to respond to a college's offer. Moreover, a last-minute acceptance often comes with less-than-ideal news on the financial aid front. In most cases, your student will now have in hand an acceptance from one of his original top-choice colleges, but without any significant financial aid. This can be quite a dilemma for many families—especially if a lower-ranked college that accepted your child in April also offered him a generous aid package.

What should you do? If you and your family succeeded in listening to each other's views of a good college match when you thoroughly discussed the available options back in April, you will simply need to do the same thing again—but in a much shorter time.

MID-YEAR ACCEPTANCES

College administrators have come to recognize that there are generally more students on campus in the fall semester than during the spring semester, when larger numbers of students tend to study abroad. In order to increase tuition income and fill empty dorm beds, many colleges now promote mid-year admission for freshmen. Applicants can be offered this mid-year admission option either in April or when they come off a wait list.

This can be a benefit to your child. Students who are accepted for mid-year admission are invited to join the freshman class at the beginning of the second semester, usually in mid-January. During the fall semester, these almost-enrolled students can work, study at another educational institution, or go overseas through any number of study abroad programs.

If your child is invited to join a college mid-year, think seriously about encouraging him to do so—especially if that institution is still one of his top choices. It would be preferable, of course, to be able to begin college with most of his classmates, but given the choice of not going to that school at all or entering second semester, the answer may be clear if your child has strong feelings about wanting to go to that particular college.

There's a big hitch, though, if your child chooses to attend another educational institution during the first semester. Some colleges don't give complete academic credit for courses taken elsewhere before students matriculate at their "home" institution. Thus, mid-year freshmen may perceive that they have no other choice than to enroll in one of the college's own study abroad programs for one semester or work at a job after high school graduation until January. Many mid-year students who choose to work in the fall ultimately catch up with their classmates by taking a full load of summer school courses after their freshman or sophomore year.

> ~There's no longer a stigma attached to the option of taking time off before starting college.~

Another possible hitch is housing. Are mid-year entrants guaranteed campus housing? Will the good housing already be taken by the time your son or daughter arrives on campus?

There is a silver lining as well. Often mid-year freshmen become a tight-knit group as a result of living together and navigating their new campus four months after other freshmen have done so.

DEFERRING FOR A YEAR

For some students, taking a year off before attending college can be a positive choice. There's no longer a stigma attached to the option of taking time off before starting college. In fact, there are a number of excellent year-long gap programs specifically designed for students who need a break before going to college. Some of these programs are overseas; some are at boarding schools in the United States; and some are specifically geared to students with particular academic interests or learning difficulties. For many teenagers, a good internship at a local company can also do just fine.

If after considering the options available in April, your child cannot see himself attending any of the colleges that accepted him, then everyone should give some thought to exploring a gap year. This was precisely the situation that Robert faced a few years ago. He was a "C" student at a California high school who was admitted to three colleges, none of which greatly excited him. He decided that he would do some organized community service work instead of going straight on to college. This turned out to be the right decision. He matured considerably during the year, and because he was now a much more sophisticated and attractive applicant, he was admitted to more desirable colleges in the admissions cycle the following year.

Other students decide to take time off simply because they want to explore some special interests before moving on to full-time college life. Emily was a top student at a well-regarded Philadelphia high school. She was accepted by almost all of the colleges to which she applied and happily accepted an offer to attend an elite Northeastern college. However, upon reflection, she decided she wanted to continue developing her interest in photography. She asked the college if she could defer for a year. The school agreed, and Emily embarked on a year-long project involving avant-garde photos of daily life in different city neighborhoods. She began college a year later with both a professional quality portfolio in hand and a rejuvenated spirit.

TRANSFERRING

We have one final comment about college selection. Remember that transferring remains an option. Of course, it's not a preferred outcome, as we all want our children to be deliciously thrilled at whatever college they choose, but you should keep the option of transferring on the table. We don't encourage your child to enter a college knowing he plans to leave after one or two semesters. However, if he is not accepted by a school to which he is passionately attached, he can start thinking about transferring the following year. Meanwhile, he can begin college and plan to have whatever credits he earns transfer with him. Once again, we urge you and your child to focus on the options currently available. Almost always there are solid colleges to choose from where your son or daughter can be truly happy.

14

Moving On:
The Big Transition

By May 1st, when most college decisions have to be made, your family will need to begin confronting the next issue, which is the adjustment to your child leaving home. This will inevitably lead to a powerful mixture of emotions on everyone's part.

COMMON TEENAGE BEHAVIOR BEFORE LEAVING FOR COLLEGE

Adolescents may feel thrilled about their impending departure, but once it's real—money deposited, roommates assigned, courses selected, and departure dates established—families often report that their teenagers suddenly become sweet and more involved with the family than they have been for years. Stories abound about teens who want to be kissed goodnight, voluntarily hang out with parents, spend time with younger siblings, and generally become home-bodies. Suddenly, it seems as if they're not ready to relinquish their childhood. Developmentally, this is certainly okay; don't assume this moderately regressive behavior means your adolescent isn't ready for college.

The approach of fall and your teenager's freshman year of college tend to elicit many feelings relating to loss. There's the inevitability of your child's recognizing the end of childhood, the stability she's known, and the comfort of being taken care of by parents unconditionally. You may start to confront your household's impending childlessness.

Many parents evaluate their own lives, often as a part of an overall midlife assessment. They see themselves as no longer primarily defined by the role of active parent. This change raises issues of aging, mortality, and the health of their marriage.

Changes in the course of our lives involve, by necessity, some form of loss. While these changes may not be experienced primarily as negative, there is still a loss. During the transition period prior to adolescents leaving for college, both parents and teenagers tend to anticipate freedom and excitement as well as loneliness and sadness. Don't be taken by surprise when you experience any or all of these conflicting emotions.

The opportunity to make new friends, create a new social circle, study new academic subjects, learn independent self-care (e.g., budgeting time, learning how to say "no" to certain temptations, doing laundry, paying bills) can simultaneously sound fabulous and terrifying to teenagers. These conflicting feelings also can lead to regression.

> ∾During the transition period prior to adolescents leaving for college, both parents and teenagers tend to anticipate freedom and excitement as well as loneliness and sadness.∾

You may have a teenager who becomes more compliant and attached to family, or you may have a teenager who starts to act out her conflicts. Acting out may take the form of disobedience, such as breaking curfew, engaging in substance experimentation, or other inappropriate or dysfunctional behavior. While you're basking in all the positive emotions, be on the lookout for these possible behaviors.

IMPORTANT CONVERSATIONS TO HAVE WITH YOUR CHILD

Living Arrangements

An issue that may have already been determined by the college search and selection process is where your child will be living in the fall. If she has chosen to attend an out-of-town college, she will have to live somewhere away from home. Generally, that means she will live in a dormitory at least for her freshman year. Students at some point may choose to live off-campus, but that's a discussion that will usually take place in a year or two.

If your child decides to attend a college within roughly fifty miles of home, you may need to consider where your child will reside. Even if a school is within commuting distance, many families support the idea of their child living on or near campus. To some, the college experience feels incomplete without a student's living on her own. If your family has the financial resources and you believe your teenager has the maturity or potential to gain the maturity to live independently, then it's certainly worthwhile to explore living options at or near her new school. A family discussion becomes necessary, however, if either the money is not readily available or if you have concerns about your child's ability to make good decisions on her own.

Are you and your student willing to trade her experience of independent living, at least for the first year or two, in order to reduce the overall cost of her college education? Not only are dormitory fees often quite high, meal plans can run into thousands of dollars each year. But, if your child lives at home, there will still be expenses, including transportation, which can be costly as well.

Money considerations aside, consider the other pros and cons of your child being a commuter student. If you're concerned about your student's ability to focus on her schoolwork while surrounded nonstop by other students and a lot of dormitory activity, then commuting may be a reasonable option. However, you can also look upon your child's living away from home as an opportunity for her to learn to focus and better manage her time. If she isn't given that chance, it may be hard for her to learn the skill. If your son or daughter has a specific handicap—physical, emotional, or educational—then this discussion becomes even more crucial. Can or should you allow your student to test the waters? What happens if she is not as successful as you and she had hoped? Is it better to try and maybe fail than to never try?

Additional considerations about commuting involve the safety of your student. Will she be driving or using public transportation late at night? Are the neighborhoods around the campus safe? Parents usually worry about their adolescents more if they're still living at home. You might wait up until your daughter comes home at night, and you'll certainly be more involved in her daily activities than you would be if she were living elsewhere. There's some truth to the adage about being out of sight and out of mind. If your child isn't living under your roof, you don't have to be as attentive, on a daily basis, to her comings and goings.

Establishing New Guidelines

Parents often struggle with how to develop new and appropriate areas of independence for their teenagers. In the process of establishing these guidelines, you all will have to create new roles within your family system.

The gradual transition of power and authority away from parents usually begins about the time teenagers graduate from high school. Students are no longer kids, but they're not totally grown up either. When your student returns home for vacation, will old rules and other limits still be appropriate or not? In either case, both parties need to learn how to have adult-to-adult relationships.

You've had the last word for years about finances, time management, telephone calls, access to the Internet, and the car. As your adolescent begins to plan for the day-to-day specifics of college living, you should start talking with her about independent living skills. An educational conversation about checking accounts, online banking, timely bill paying, and credit cards may ease her way.

It's useful to identify banks that are on or near campus. If possible, use a bank that has a branch near your home and another near your daughter's college. This way, she can have access to her account at both locations, and you, too, can access the account conveniently.

You'll need to be specific about how much money you or she will be allocating for expenditures each month. You may want to develop a budget, in which you factor in books and supplies, additional food purchases (which will vary depending on the meal plan you selected), entertainment, and other incidentals. Before your son or daughter leaves for college, decide how expenses will be paid. Will she use her own account? Will she be able to use a family credit card? What will she be allowed to charge?

Maintaining Contact

A topic that's frequently overlooked is how each family plans to maintain contact once their teenager leaves for college. Some questions to consider ahead of time are easily framed. Will your daughter be expected to call home or will you be calling her? Will regular e-mails, phone calls, text messages, or letters be expected? Planning how your family will stay in touch will help ease everyone's anxiety about staying connected. Often, if students contact parents on a regular basis, the parents—and siblings—are reassured of their connection.

Keeping in touch with family and friends from home is important for your child, but she also needs time to develop relationships in her new environment. She should expend most of her social energies on creating a group of friends at college.

How do you manage this balancing act of maintaining contact while encouraging new connections? Discuss this issue directly. Try to hear what your child may be telling you—not just the words themselves, but the underlying message. You can encourage her to seek out new relationships while being supportive of her need, and yours as well, to maintain good rapport with those back home.

Trips Back Home During School Breaks

Anticipate what might happen during parents' weekends and school breaks. Plan ahead and discuss your expectations. Parents are often hurt that they don't seem as important to their children any more. On parents' visiting weekend, students often "abandon" their folks to engage in peer activities. Deciding when, where, and with whom you all plan to gather can be helpful.

Can you budget for your student to fly home during fall break and Thanksgiving, as well as winter break? What about other visits home for family events, such as birthdays or weddings?

Even though you may be willing, whatever the cost, to have your student come home, she may sometimes elect not to. How will you cope? Is it okay for her to remain at school for some breaks? What if she wants to go to her roommate's house for Thanksgiving or travel elsewhere for winter break? Consider these options and possibilities carefully before your teenager leaves for school in August or September. Think about your feelings, and how these options resonate with you. Then talk to your child about a possible plan.

Lay out some scenarios and establish some potential ground rules before freshman year begins. It's much easier to discuss these issues face-to-face and in advance than to have to quickly negotiate these emotionally charged decisions later.

THE SUMMER BEFORE FRESHMAN YEAR

After all the high school work, college decisions, and graduation, it's now time to plan for the next stage of the transition. When you learn the college-orientation dates, work backward through your family's schedule. Leave time to shop and pack several days before the trek to college. Then figure out if your family can take a vacation together. Try to go to a place where everyone can relax and enjoy one another's company. This may be a location that you go to regularly or someplace you've been meaning to travel to for a long time.

Make sure you have the opportunity to keep family traditions, such as eating at favorite restaurants, taking familiar walks, or talking about positive childhood experiences. Ask your child what she most wants to do over the summer. Although she may have a job and you may be working a full schedule, carve out time for these activities.

Interweave discussions about the past with those about the present and future. Make sure you don't dwell just on the past or just on the future. Total emphasis on either may lead you or your child to feel too nostalgic or anxious about the impending separation. Enjoy being in the moment.

EASING THE TRANSITION INTO THE FIRST SEMESTER

Children of all ages need to be reassured that there will always be a place for them at home—even if they don't plan to return often. College-bound students may fret that younger siblings will usurp their bedrooms. They worry that mom and dad might get rid of their stuff. Or most seriously, will mom and dad move to a new and possibly smaller house?

During the first semester of Olivia's freshman year, her parents announced that they had sold their home and were moving to a new townhouse. The freshman was told she would have a basement apartment of her own in the townhouse when she returned for vacation. While on some level this arrangement may have sounded attractive, and it would certainly appeal to a young woman's sense of independence and maturity, the parents were oblivious to their daughter's feelings of being emotionally cut off.

Make sure you have a discussion regarding your child's bedroom before she sets off for college. Try to keep her space intact for at least her freshman year. If this isn't possible, the next best thing is to discuss any changes ahead of time. Where will "her space" be in your home and where will you put her possessions?

Parents must walk a fine line between respecting their children's growing independence and maturity, and not emotionally kicking them out of the house too quickly. The need to belong remains, despite the departure for college. This delicate push and pull is experienced by most parents and their teens. We simultaneously yearn for closeness to our children, but we also understand from our own experiences the desire for independence from parents. Your child wants to be close but also wants her space.

A further source of family unease may involve your daughter's siblings. Younger brothers and sisters may be feeling neglected after all the focus on your college-bound student. At some point, they may feel rebellious and make it clear that they want your time and attention too. But few teenagers give up the spotlight readily, and your college-bound child may not be happy about passing on this attention before she leaves for school.

～Make sure you have a discussion regarding your child's bedroom before she sets off for college.～

To further prepare for the transition to college life, take some time to consider how you will deal with stressful situations that may arise during your child's first semester. Having some anticipation of what those emotional bumps might be can be extremely helpful. You may find it valuable to set up a tentative plan to address emotional upheavals, should any materialize.

There are numerous areas of social stress that can affect your child during her first weeks away at college. One common occurrence is not getting along with a roommate. For some students, this is merely a minor inconvenience. They are teenagers who find it easy to make friends wherever they go and are quite comfortable with who they are. They don't seek validation from a roommate, and they're able to compartmentalize their feelings about their living situation.

For other students, not getting along with a roommate can be devastating. Given the huge build-up of excitement and anticipation, a student can be dramatically disappointed if she doesn't socially or emotionally connect with a roommate. There's not much advance planning you can do for this situation other than being prepared to be supportive of your child. Mostly, you'll need to help your child cope with the disappointment and annoyance of not getting along with someone in close proximity. However, there are some situations that are clearly intolerable, like a roommate who has a substance abuse problem, or a roommate who has a sleep-in boyfriend or girlfriend. If these scenarios occur, encourage your child to change rooms.

~To further prepare for the transition to college life, take some time to consider how you will deal with stressful situations that may arise during your child's first semester.~

Early in the first semester of college, your daughter may complain about not having enough new friends or not going out frequently. She may bemoan the separation from her high school friends. Encourage her to keep moving forward and not keep looking back.

Your teenager, especially if she has led a sheltered life throughout high school, may be disturbed by the variety and degree of lifestyle differences that she may encounter at college. You and she may have already discussed these issues while visiting campuses. Usually, though, it doesn't really hit home until your student is living the experience. She may be dismayed by alcohol use, attitudes toward sexual relationships, and different views about school and work. Encourage your student to acknowledge these differences and try to help her feel less isolated.

Help your child figure out how to meet students with whom she may share some things in common. Also acknowledge, however, that learning to deal with people from whom we are quite different can be an exciting and enriching experience. Just because you meet and associate with people different from yourself doesn't mean you need to become more like them.

Another stressor, both for you and your child, may be her initial academic performance. Be prepared for a possible rocky road in this arena during the first semester. Your child may not be used to the style of teaching at college, or she may not be prepared for the amount of independent study required for her to do well. Also, many top high school students find that when they get to college, they're no longer big fish in a small pond. They are no longer at the top of the class or they have to work harder to stay there. This change can be a blow to the ego, as well as a letdown regarding expectations for a high GPA.

Before your child goes off to school, you may want to discuss how she can find academic support. Can she get help from a professor or teaching assistant? Can she find a study group or create one herself? Can she seek out help from an on-campus counseling service? Are the courses she selected to take first semester a reasonable course load? Or is she biting off more than she can chew, given the distractions of freshman college life? Be aware that colleges no longer send grades home to parents. They're sent only to your student. So it's a good idea to speak with your child ahead of time about how she will share her grades with you.

If you find that your student starts complaining loudly about her adjustment to college life, you should listen carefully. It's hard, especially from a distance, to determine if your child is truly unhappy or if she's just using you as a safe sounding board. Continue to be a good listener, asking for clarification when needed and being supportive of your child's struggle. Be careful, though, not to encourage these complaints too much. Use your knowledge of your child to assess if she's just learning to adjust or if she's truly floundering. If the latter is the case, you may start hearing rumblings about wanting to transfer to a different college. Listen to the rationale, be open to possibilities, but also encourage your student to keep working at making her present experience better. Even if your child ultimately decides to change colleges, you want her to gain as much socially, emotionally, and academically from her first year as she can.

LOOKING FORWARD

You and your spouse should make sure to discuss what life will be like when your child goes away to college. Certainly, you will want to include in the discussion all children who are still remaining at home. Be prepared for shifts in power, including who will now have the role of oldest sibling, and possible shifts in the use of space in the home.

If there are no other children left at home, you and your spouse should discuss what it may feel like—both from a positive and a negative vantage point. Plan trips or other joint activities to take the edge off the feeling of an empty house. This may be the time to explore new hobbies or to become more involved in old interests. Congratulate yourselves on how successful you have been as parents. You've done a good job in launching your child toward a bright future at a college of her choosing. Now is the time to revel in your accomplishments and look forward to your own futures and how you plan to craft them.

FINAL THOUGHTS

Throughout this book, we've stressed the importance of being sensitive to each other's needs and points of view. The college admissions process, like many other family growth and childrearing experiences, can be demanding and filled with anxiety. Nonetheless, it's only a part of the journey, and although significant, it's essential to keep it in perspective.

Your family and the strength of its relationships will be tested by both the admissions process and other important life-cycle events. We encourage each member of your family to be a resource for one another—and to view your child's quest for the right college as a source of strength that will cement the bonds of your family for years to come.

Index

About the Authors

Steven Roy Goodman, MS, JD (www.topcolleges.com), has designed admissions strategies for more than 1,500 applicants to colleges, graduate programs, and business, law, and medical schools. He helps students and families with educational planning, internships, summer activities, gap programs, study abroad, transfer applications, interview training, and campus visits. He is a frequent expert source for journalists, and his op-eds have been published in the *Washington Post*, the *Philadelphia Inquirer*, the *Miami Herald*, and other media outlets. He is a former faculty member of the Wharton School and Haverford College.

Andrea Leiman, PhD, is a clinical psychologist and professor. She teaches courses in family therapy and the psychology of interpersonal relations. She has twenty-five years of experience working with families in psychotherapy and strengthening family relationships. In addition to providing diagnostic psychological testing, she has covered a broad spectrum of psychotherapeutic modalities in her practice. She offers individual therapy for children, adolescents, adults, and couples, as well as consultation to parent groups, organizations, and school staffs on issues of child development.